BLOOD
BROTHERHOOD

AND OTHER RITES
OF MALE ALLIANCE

2ND REVISED EDITION

NATHAN F. MILLER
JACK DONOVAN

DISSONANT HUM

OREGON

Second Edition, Revised

First Edition published in print 2009 by Jack Donovan
ISBN-10: 0578030705
ISBN-13: 978-0578030708

Second Edition electronically published 2011 by Jack Donovan [Dissonant Hum]
ASIN: B005FLU4ZA

Second Edition published in print 2013 by Jack Donovan [Dissonant Hum]
ISBN-10: 0985452323
ISBN-13: 978-0-9854523-2-2

Cover Design and Artwork by Jack Donovan.

[DISSONANT HUM]

4230 SE King Road, No. 185
Milwaukie, Oregon. 97222
USA.

www.dissonant-hum.com

Subjects:

1. Social Sciences - Men's Studies
2. Psychology - Men
4. Men - Social Conditions
5. Masculinity - History
6. Sex role
7. Gender Studies

CONTENTS

A TIMELESS WAY
TO FORGE BONDS BETWEEN MEN

BY JACK DONOVAN

Blood-brotherhood is probably almost as old as brotherhood itself. There's something archetypal about it, something that echoes and reverberates through human history. It maintains a certain resonance with men even in our own times, although blood has been stripped of the magical qualities attributed to it by our ancestors and science has revealed that even as the blood flowing through our veins carries nutrients and life to our cells, blood can also be the bringer of disease and death.

The desire to create blood-brotherhood seems to be a natural outgrowth of male friendship, an acknowledgement of the simple fact that men often develop bonds with men outside their biological family just as they do with their own kin. It is an answer to the question, "Why should we, too, not be brothers?" Blood-brotherhood extends the biological family; it creates a meta-family—a family beyond family. It borrows from the emotional range natural to brotherhood—loyalty, camaraderie, mutually understood trust, and a sense of mutual empathy and attachment based on shared history, experiences and interests. In recognition of the fact that the same emotions can be shared between men who are not related by blood, blood-brotherhood extends many of the privileges of brotherhood to a male friend. While in some cultures blood-brotherhood is a political gesture, in other cultures the practice of making blood-brothers is the acknowledgment of a very real, intense friendship between otherwise unrelated men. The status, privileges and loyalty accorded to a blood-brother often surpassed those of a biological brother. In fact, blood-brotherhoods were often so important that they took precedence over all other human connections, including marriage.

Blood-brotherhood as the ritualized acknowledgment of male friendship and the creation of a "spiritual brotherhood" is the focus of this survey.

Male friendship in the early 21st century West is a sensitive topic buried in alternating layers of irony and silence. It is often misunderstood and susceptible to poor analysis. Masculine friendship is often a quiet, mutual understanding, expressed through deeds and sincere gestures. It is an agreement between men, not something to shout about in the town square with dramatic outpourings of affection. In most cases it is of greater importance to the men involved than it is to anyone else, though if the men are good friends that fact is usually understood by the people around them. Male friendship is usually a storyline layered beneath the tales of men—a sub-plot—as it is portrayed in many cinematic Westerns and war films. This book provides many exceptions to this general rule, stories wherein strong bonds of friendship between men are formalized among friends or even publicly. However, the character of these rites of friendship between men remains wholly masculine and the honor of the men involved is uncompromised. Blood-brotherhood is a social institution which, like the modern Australian tradition of "mateship" and the European/American "fraternity," remains exempt from taboos concerning the public expressions of affection between men, largely because it is grounded in a masculine aesthetic and in a masculine understanding of things.

In most cultures it is permissible for a man to show fascination with and love for a woman. It is common for men to make complete fools of themselves in an effort to demonstrate the sincerity of their emotions and affection for a woman in order to win her favor. The moment where a man puts aside his dignity and throws himself at the foot of his beloved is the climax of countless tales of romantic love, new and old. But to put aside honor for a woman fits into the scheme of things precisely because she is a woman. A woman in the context of courtship symbolizes emotion and sensitivity and the delicacy of feminine beauty. Because men and women are essentially different, wanting different things and operating under a different set of social rules and expectations, there is no real conflict of status or honor within the context of male/female courtship. When a man puts his dignity aside and gushes emotionally to win the favor of a woman, it is rightly the subject of joking and teasing among men, and significantly, not among women, but unless his behavior is extreme he loses no status or esteem. Most men know they have done or will do the same thing; most women pine for it. The presence of a woman in the equation is the motivation and the excuse for his atypical behavior.

When men express a strong attachment for one another, because there is no immediately evident distinction of social roles between them, no obvious polarity between male and female, no obvious appeals to be made to the natural insanity of hard-wired mating instincts—the rules of engagement are different. If the romantic drama of courtship between men and women is the only model, the effect is psychological emasculation of one or both parties. When no woman is present to demand or excuse the lapse of honor and dignity associated with emotional displays resembling courtship behavior, it seems natural—if a bit unfair—to attribute a feminine element to the men involved.

When men express a strong emotional bond between each other, they must remain men. Overt gestures of submission to a woman are part of the mating game that men and women play, but overt gestures of submission to another man are counterintuitive—they signal defeat, dishonor and weakness. A man admires his friend, but he may not *lose himself* in that admiration to the extent that he appears to be completely *enthralled*. In the context of male friendship, one man is often the leader and the other the follower or "sidekick." There is often a natural alpha and beta, but if both parties don't respect each other as men and regard each other as such, it's not much of a friendship at all; the friendship is one-sided, exploitative and dishonorable. In strong male friendships, while the men involved may have similar (and therefore competitive) natural aptitudes, they recognize each other's manhood, independent will and personal sovereignty. As we will see throughout our exploration of blood-brotherhood, it is usually one of the primary duties of a blood-brother to defend his friend's honor. To express this sort of friendship and camaraderie in an emasculating way is contradictory to the spirit of male friendship. A strong emotional bond between men should affirm the masculinity and honor of the men involved—not call it into question.

Blood-brotherhood is one recurring cultural solution to the problem of recognizing powerful emotional bonds between men that avoids effeminizing comparisons to romantic courtship and affirms the masculinity of the men involved. Blood-brotherhoods, which could be seen as the ultimate expression of male friendship, have been celebrated in myth, art, literature and in common practice across a wide variety of cultures, on every populated continent of the Earth, for thousands of years.

The practice has been particularly well-documented by historians and anthropologists in Africa, where it was ritualized in a variety of ways from culture to culture. There is evidence of blood-brotherhood amongst the tribes of Australia and the Pacific islands. The practice of exchanging names, a comparable male friendship ritual, was common in Tahiti and the Marquesas Islands. This inspired author Jack London to write a short story about a name-exchange pact between a white American and a "black kanaka heathen" from Bora Bora. Writers of American pioneer novels and Westerns have fermented myths about blood-brotherhood practices among Native Americans, and as such, the idea of blood-brotherhood pacts between "Injuns" and Caucasians has become a part of American lore. The Lone Ranger and his loyal sidekick Tonto were blood-brothers. Karl May, a German author of American Westerns, wrote novels about a German adventurer and his Apache blood-brother, Winnetou, that are still popular in Germany today. Tom Sawyer made a secret blood pact with Huckleberry Finn in Mark Twain's *The Adventures of Tom Sawyer*. The Celtic *Ulster Cycle* tells of a blood-brotherhood between the heroic warriors Cúchulainn and Ferdiad. In Norse mythology, the *Lokasenna* described a blood-brotherhood between Odin and Loki. Heroes Gunther and Siegfried performed a sacred rite of blood-brotherhood in the fourth opera of Richard Wagner's famous *Der Ring des Nibelungen* cycle. The *Ring* cycle itself was based on the Medieval German *Niebelungenlied*, *The Poetic Edda*, and the Icelandic *Völsunga Saga*, the latter two of which also contain a version of the blood-brotherhood. There is documented evidence of blood-brotherhood from Ancient Egypt, and the classical historians

Herodotus, Xenophon and Sallust wrote of various blood pacts, blood oaths and blood-brotherhoods in Ancient Greece and Rome. Blood-brotherhood also figured in Serbian legends of Prince Marko Kraljevich. In Asia, the great conqueror Genghis Khan had a famously conflicted relationship with his childhood blood-brother.

Blood-bonding is, with relatively few exceptions, a male practice. Although there is some evidence of "blood-sisterhood" between two women, among the Mongols for instance, and blood rites were sometimes a component of marriage ceremonies between men and women, the vast majority of material documenting blood-bonds describe them as agreements between male friends and comrades. The idea of blood-sisterhood is rare and isolated, whereas blood-brotherhood, as noted above, is a persistent cross-cultural human phenomenon.

What is it about mutual cutting and the sharing of blood that has inspired men from diverse cultures and geographical regions to employ this method of solemnizing their friendships and alliances? What qualities give blood-brotherhood its masculine character and have made it so uniquely attractive to men over the millennia?

Perhaps it is because, for the majority of its history, manhood has been a bloody business. The role of men has traditionally been to hunt, to fight, to defend, to make war. To be a man was to risk blood, to draw blood. The world of men has always been a grisly reality, and the right to call oneself a man has often been earned by showing courage and facing this reality head-on, in battle or during the hunt. Men struggle with nature and other men to carve out some measure of calm for the women who bear the next generation of men. Womanhood is also a bloody business; menstrual blood is a powerful female symbol and childbirth is a bloody mess. However, this blood flows naturally, as part of biological processes. The blood of manhood is blood that is *drawn* through *action*, with *intent*. As a sacred element, blood represents a man's dominance over nature, over other men, over himself.

In British author William Golding's *The Lord of the Flies,* one of the boys marks his forehead with blood of the first pig killed by his hunting party.[1] This is probably an allusion to the practice of "blooding," which was common in Great Britain until recently. According to tradition, youths out hunting for the first time were daubed on the cheeks or the forehead with the still warm blood of the quarry—usually a fox, a stag or a game bird.[2] Analogous hunting traditions have been noted in Mongolia and Russia.[3] Among the !Kung people of Africa, a boy who has killed his first eland, a kind of antelope, is cut, and the wound is rubbed with the fat and hair of the beast. The resulting scar is a symbol of his status as a hunter. [4]

Several accounts portray the ancient Celts as having drunk the blood of their enemies and rubbed it on their faces, presumably to gain the enemy's strength. The ancient Celts were also thought to have drunk the blood of their dead relatives in an effort to gain their virtues and bring them closer in spirit to the departed. In his 1911 study of Celtic religion, J.A. MacCulloch makes the connection between these practices and the practice of making blood-brotherhood, also popular among the Celts.[5] It is worth noting here the similarity between partaking of blood to unite with the dead, and sharing blood to unite the living. Using this example, blood-brotherhood could be viewed as an attempt between two men to share one another's strengths and virtues.

Blood-brotherhood is not for the faint of heart. The premeditated infliction of a wound for ritual purposes calls to mind tribal "toughness tests" that demonstrate manliness and self-discipline and precede initiations into groups of men. For examples of such tests we could reach for fare such as the foreskin chewing adolescent circumcision rites of the Selako Dayak people of Borneo[6] or the painful genital tattooing of young Samoan men.[7] But such exotic and extreme examples are not necessary; we could just as easily refer to fraternity hazing or modern gang initiation. Toughness testing remains a routine feature of male-to-male socialization. Any male reading this has probably been put in a position where he was expected to prove his masculinity by "manning up" and enduring pain, hard work, discomfort or at the very least a bit of razzing, or he has dished it out. It is fitting that men making a commitment to one another should endure pain in the process—with each man proving his sincerity, his worthiness and affirming his masculinity. A blood-brotherhood here could be interpreted as a ritual initiation into a fraternity of two.

Knives, spears and other cutting implements figure prominently in many blood-brotherhood rites. This is in part for utilitarian reasons—you need something to break the skin and draw blood. But a knife is a weapon, a tool, and a phallic symbol. Knives evoke some of the most important, sex-specific roles that men have played in traditional societies where men were hunters, warriors and builders. It is a natural choice to employ knives or similar tools or weapons in a ritual that bonds two men.

Lionel Tiger originated the popular term "male bonding." In *Men in Groups,* he asserts that "males bond in terms of either a pre-existent object of aggression, or a concocted one."[8] It makes sense that men who wanted to ritualize a bond of friendship would incorporate elements of hunting or war-making into their rites. Historically, close male friendships were probably formed during warfare or hunting. In our relatively peaceful society where a majority of adult males are not required to hunt or make war, these aggressive tendencies are channeled into sports or video games or action movies or martial arts. Modern men often bond over simulated aggression, or less obvious forms of aggression that also fit Tiger's model—activities which require a triumph over nature (outdoor sports like hiking, rock climbing, white water rafting) or over a mutual problem or project (building or fixing something) or a perceived foe (bonding over politics, for example). Drawing blood, symbolic of primal aggression, remains resonant and relevant for men even in our age of sublimated aggression. We may not all be hunters and warriors, but we need only look to the names of modern sports teams, or to the marketing of the most popular products and forms of entertainment for men to recognize the powerful atavistic draw of these ancient archetypal roles.

There is probably no single reason why men in so many cultures have found themselves attracted to the idea of blood-brotherhood, and there is no evidence to suggest that the tradition came from a single source or was transmitted from culture to culture. Rather, what we have in blood-brotherhood is a method of recognizing male friendships and alliances that employs the drawing of blood to draw from a deep well of essentially masculine imagery and symbolism and affirms the masculinity of the participants.

The bulk of this book is a collection of myths, histories and stories about blood-brotherhood and similar forms of created brotherhood. It is a survey of male friendships and alliances, in communities that recognized the unique character and gravity of bonds between men. It is our hope in presenting this information that men will find inspiration in this survey of blood-brotherhood. We hope that the myths, stories and practices of men who came before them will provide readers with a context that will enrich their own friendships.

A TOOLBOX FOR THE IMAGINATION – MEANING AND METHODOLOGY

Blood-Brotherhood is designed as a "toolbox for the imagination." The wide range of historical, mythological and literary examples collected in this volume are intended to inspire and serve as a reference points for men seeking a masculine context for their bonds, and for men in the process of customizing or constructing their own rituals. Stories and traditions associated with blood-brotherhood may give men who have long-standing bonds new ways to think about their relationships and add new layers of meaning to their enduring mutual loyalty and sense of family.

This project does not codify the exact rules, symbols and ritual practices for one type of bond and present that bond as an ideal superior to all others. There is no "one size fits all" plan here. Our intent is to present a variety of source material related to blood-brotherhood—a collection of stories, ideas and methods to be used as raw materials and tools by men who want to build their own traditions from the ground up, according to their own individual needs, preferences and tastes. This "build-your-own-bond" approach is consistent with many traditions of blood-brotherhood, where participants made up their own vows to one another. As one researcher of African blood-brotherhoods wrote, "Blood-brotherhood was to create idealized relations between men. [...] it was a specific form of filiation and intimacy that was under individual male control." [9]

Indeed, while other bonding institutions, such as marriage, are usually conducted by a priest or shaman of some kind, blood-brotherhood rites were most often performed by the men themselves. A blood-brotherhood is something between a spiritual bond and a contract. Instead of employing a third party to act as a medium or celebrant, blood bonds have relied on the will and the spiritual authority of the participants.

Blood-brotherhood is both a way to define an ideal, and to make sure certain rules, commitments and obligations are mutually understood. The terms are negotiable, and they vary from culture to culture, but the recurring themes of trust, loyalty, mutual appreciation and respect are worth highlighting at the outset of our survey.

TRUST + LOYALTY

Blood-brotherhood has been used ceremonially by chiefs and leaders to unite groups of people. As part of an alliance or treaty, it symbolically creates a familial bond, communicating trust and loyalty. Allied tribes or states, while retaining their separate identities and their independence, are expected to support one another in conflict, to favor one another according to the terms of their agreement, and to assist one another whenever possible. The groups become more formidable as a result of their combined strengths. When the agreement is formalized, the groups in question can rest assured they no longer stand alone, because their allies have "got their backs."

The same is essentially true for men at the individual level. The main reason to formalize a relationship or a friendship is to confirm a sense of mutual trust and loyalty. A man needs to know who his friends are. It is not enough to *hope* your pal has "got your back." It is better to *know* it. A man wants to *know* that his friend is bound (by honor or supernatural forces, or both) to stand by his side when he's in need.

One of the consistent features of blood-brotherhood pacts across cultures is the promise of mutual aid; blood-brothers vow to remain loyal to each other. In some cultures, blood-brothers were more important than "milk-brothers" —brothers from the same mother—and were expected to stand up for one another even against their own families if necessary. The sealing of an alliance between great warriors, who would vow to fight together for one another to the death if necessary, is a common theme in myths involving blood-brotherhood. Blood pacts have often been used to initiate individuals into secret societies or to bind men together in conspiracy, where allegiance to the goals and secrets of the group were to be maintained even in instances of capture or torture. In some tribes, blood-brothers were expected to help each other evade the authorities in cases of murder, even if the perpetrator was in the wrong. Sometimes a man would lay down his life for his blood-brother, or offer to be executed in his place. Often, there has been a sense that the fate of blood-brothers is linked, and in a few instances, blood-brothers were expected to follow each other into death.

Other responsibilities of blood-brothers have included the execution of a deceased brother's will. Some traditions of blood-brotherhood created a sense of communal property between the brothers, or brothers were entrusted with the care of each other's most valuable property. In some instances, blood-brothers agreed to share women or wives. In others, a pact of blood-brotherhood included a promise not to commit adultery with a blood-brother's wife. A theme common to many myths involving blood-brotherhood is that competition over women or sex often leads to the betrayal of a blood-brotherhood, and the eventual ruin of both men.

Many blood-brotherhood pacts involved a curse as a penalty for betrayal. Some rituals have involved the reading of lists of horrific torments to befall the brother who broke the oath in "word, thought or deed." Some men believed that the blood itself would take vengeance upon the betrayer, causing sickness or death. In African rituals that involved the ingestion of coffee beans, it was believed that the beans would "swell up" and kill the traitor. It is safe to assume that most sworn-brothers expected a brother who betrayed him in some way to get what he deserved, and suffer for it.

Whether between two men or between groups of men, rites of blood-brotherhood establish a mutual sense of allegiance. A blood-brother is symbolically entrusted with the things most important to a man, from his property to his life.

MUTUAL APPRECIATION + RESPECT

In *The Epic of Gilgamesh*, one of the oldest pieces of human literature, Gilgamesh meets his foster brother Enkidu in conflict. The two fight until, according to some interpretations of the myth, they find that they are evenly matched, and decide to become friends and eventually become foster-brothers. There is a similar theme in Arthurian mythology. Knights frequently meet in battle and fight until they are both spent, at which point, out of mutual respect, they become great friends.

Blood-brotherhood is usually a bond between two men on equal terms. This feature distinguishes it from biological brotherhood, in which there is often a hierarchy of seniority. It also differentiates blood-brotherhood from other unions, such as traditional marriage, where the two parties assume different roles and the man is expected to wield authority over the woman. A blood-brother does not take a subservient position in the relationship; he is an ally who enters the agreement independently, of his own free will and on his own terms. He is expected to remain a man, and blood-brothers must respect each other as men. There is no requirement that the two brothers must be evenly matched in every sense, but each maintains a certain amount of personal sovereignty. Blood-brothers remain men with their own interests, and as mentioned above, one of the biggest benefits of blood-brotherhood is that a friend is bound to help you protect *your own* interests and *your own* honor. Blood-brothers must mutually appreciate each other as men in their own right and respect one another's manhood, or their bond would be an exploitative sham. If you don't respect your brother's right to have his own interests, why vow to protect those interests?

Framed in terms of alliance, this sounds a bit cold and political. But why would a man choose to bond himself forever to a man whom he does not consider *worthy*? Why vow to put his life or interests on the line for a man who has not earned his respect and admiration? Why link his fate to a guy he doesn't even *like*?

In truth, these general ideas and values are essential to any good friendship. They are certainly not specific to blood-brotherhood. A blood bond is one of many ways to make a mutual commitment to hold true to certain ideals. The general themes mentioned above are presented here to capture a certain cross-cultural "spirit" of blood-brotherhood, because they are common to many blood-brotherhood traditions. Trust, loyalty, mutual appreciation and respect are key themes to consider and incorporate when crafting a blood-brotherhood.

RITUAL PRACTICE

The image of blood-brotherhood most familiar to American men seems to be the pricking and rubbing together of thumbs, or in some cases the cutting and rubbing together of hands or forearms. Yet, overall the most popular methods of creating blood-brotherhood seem to include the drinking or ingestion of mixed blood.

Where cutting is part of the ritual practice, the location of the cut might be standard within a culture, or it might suggest different levels of intimacy. A cut on the upper arm might signify strength; a cut on the forearm might be merely for political purposes. A cut near the heart, on the stomach, or on the groin could signify a more intimate relationship and a greater amount of trust. Sometimes men have cut each other, which certainly implies a great deal of trust, but in other traditions a man would merely cut himself in the sight of the other man. During some ancient Arab rites, the blood was smeared on sacred stones.

In some blood-brotherhood traditions, the two men suck the blood from each other's wounds. It is more common for men to draw blood and then mix it with wine or beer, or apply it to a piece of bread or meat or some other food item, and then eat or drink the mixed blood.

HEALTH CONCERNS

There are health-related concerns about encouraging men to re-invigorate traditions of blood-brotherhood. There is certainly a greater understanding of germs and viruses and the transmission of disease today than when blood-brotherhood traditions were initially conceived. Many diseases can be transmitted through direct blood and fluid exchanges.

That said, some perspective is in also in order. We are not advising men to go make blood-brotherhood with every man they meet. To do so would be inconsistent with the tradition and spirit of blood-brotherhood. When men join as blood-brothers they tie their fates to each other and vow to stand together no matter what. Blood-brotherhoods are not to be entered into lightly. The following passage, written by Lucian of Samosata in the second century CE, likens blood-brotherhood to a careful courtship, by emphasizing the masculinity and worthiness of the men involved.

> "Friendships are not formed with us, as with you, over the wine-cups, nor are they determined by considerations of age or neighborhood. We wait till we see a brave man, capable of valiant deeds, and to him we turn our attention. Friendship with us is like courtship with you: rather than fail of our object, and undergo the disgrace of a rejection, we are content to urge our suit patiently, and to give our constant attendance. At length a friend is accepted, and the engagement is concluded with our most solemn oath: 'to live together and if need be to die for one another.' That vow is faithfully kept: once let the friends draw blood from their fingers into a cup, dip the points of their swords therein, and drink of that draught together, and from that moment nothing can part them. Such a treaty of friendship may include three persons, but no more: a man of many friends we consider to be no better than a woman who is at the service of every lover; we feel no further security in a friendship that is divided between so many objects."[10]

Could we ask for nobler, more inspiring guidance on selecting a blood-brother?

It is this profound level of sincerity, devotion, trust and loyalty that is being advocated here. If you can not trust a blood-brother to be honest about his intentions or potential health concerns, why would you pledge your life to him?

If there is a known health concern between two men, this should be discussed. There are some blood-brotherhood traditions explored in this survey which do not involve fluid exchange at all, such as the Norse ritual, which had blood mixed into the earth. Blood-brotherhood rites have also included symbolic gestures which could be substituted for blood transfer, such as exchanging meaningful gifts, exchanging clothing, sleeping side-by-side, making oaths over a shared animal sacrifice, exchanging names, or by planting a tree together. Traditions that involve blood-drinking often call for the mixing of blood with some alcoholic beverage, and alcohol—especially in higher concentrations, as with whiskey or vodka—is known to kill many viruses and germs on contact.

The authors of this book are not health care professionals, so if you have any concerns about potential health risks involved in any blood-brotherhood ritual described in this book, please consult your physician or do your own research and proceed at your own risk.

Another alternative to the actual mixing or drinking of blood is explored in the final chapter of this book, titled "Blood and Ink." Because tattoos are so popular and so widely accepted today, some men may choose to solemnize their bonds by getting symbolic tattoos, or by tattooing each other. "Blood and Ink" discusses the masculine history of the tattoo, and presents the shared tattoo as a modern method of making blood-brotherhood.

They have looked each other between the eyes,

and there they found no fault,

They have taken the Oath of the Brother-in-Blood

on leavened bread and salt:

They have taken the Oath of the Brother-in-Blood

on fire and fresh-cut sod,

On the hilt and the haft of the Khyber knife,

and the Wondrous Names of God.

— Rudyard Kipling, "The Ballad of East and West"

RITES OF MALE ALLIANCE

BLOOD-BROTHERHOOD IN AFRICA

The historic roots of the practice of blood-brotherhood are unknown. It is uncertain whether or not the rite had a single geographic origin. However, it seems appropriate that the continent with the most widespread institution of blood-brotherhood is also the continent of mankind's own origin. Blood-brotherhood was still a common practice in Africa in the nineteenth century during the era of European exploration and colonization, so scholars and explorers were able to make many observations of the practice. Anthropologists have collected instances of the rite occurring in over 200 locations on the African continent.[1] Some have been investigated in depth. The form of the rite might vary considerably even in a single society, so it is possible that many variations in an area have never been recorded at all.

One of the better-studied blood-brotherhood customs was that of the Azande people, of the north-west part of the Central African Republic, and neighboring areas of the Congo and Sudan. The term for the relationship created by the rite was bakure, meaning "cut-blood," and a man would refer to his blood-brother as bakurëmi, "my bakure."[2] The rite was sometimes done for practical purposes such as trade agreements, and securing of safe passage through dangerous territories. More often, however, the ritual was performed between friends, replacing the vague obligations of friendship with more definite and certain rules and commitments,[3] and thus making their relationship somewhat more like kinship.

Azande men about to make blood-brotherhood would give out
very little publicity, informing only close friends and family of what
they were going to do, and a small number of these might attend the
ritual. There was considerable variation possible in the details of how
the ritual was performed. The two men sat facing each other, and cuts
were placed on the arms, or on the chest. Attending relatives might
make these cuts, or the men might mutually cut each other. Each man
then put some of the other's blood on a bit of benge wood, which he
then chewed, or else upon some groundnuts, which he then ate. This
was thought to mix the blood.[4]

A second part of the ritual delineated the oath. One man took
two knives, and continually clashed them against each other over the
other man's head, while he commanded the blood to take vengeance
if the other brother should break various obligations. This speech to
the "brother"—and the blood—could be quite itemized and lengthy.
Instead of using knives, a cord of grass or bark-fiber might be twist-
ed and untwisted over the man's head during this pronouncement.
Then the roles reversed, the second man speaking to, and about, the
first.[5] The ceremony ended with an exchange of gifts, usually of large
knives.[6]

Among the Azande of the Meridi area of Sudan, one blood-brotherhood ritual had a very different form. The men would cut each
other's foreheads, and drink each other's blood directly from the cut.
Next, each would rub a lock of the other's hair in the blood, and then
cut off the lock to keep as a charm.[7]

The obligations pronounced in the Azande blood-brother ritual
commonly included promises to share the meat of hunted game; to
readily give objects which one bakure needed and which the other
could afford to part with; not to commit adultery with the other's
wife; to give the blood-brother priority when looking for a husband
for an unmarried daughter; to give assistance against any enemies,
usually including the official powers. Once, the bakure had a grim-
mer duty: if a man had been accused of witchcraft—thought to be an
innate feature which left signs in the body—then upon his death it
was the duty of his blood-brother to open up his corpse to show that

he had normal human entrails.[8]

One result of the camaraderie of Azande blood-brothers was how it would often lead to what anthropologists term a "joking relationship." The two would get into pretend-arguments in public, exchanging inventive insults. One bakure might play practical jokes on the other. For instance, he sends the "news" of a family death to his blood-brother, who then travels off to his own home village, only to find everyone alive and well. Sometimes, whole clans might be drawn into this joking, making a sort of phony feuding for fun.[9] The language and actions are things that would be taken as offensive in an ordinary context, but because of the special relationship, no real offense is meant or taken.

Since Azande blood-brotherhood increased the connection between a man and his blood-brother's relatives, the bakure relationship might be thought of as a created kinship, but it was also different in many ways. The Azande did not think of membership in one clan as a connection of blood, but as a connection of common fathers' "seed"; the voluntarily created blood-connection was thus something more unique. As noted before the bakure relationship did not make the female relatives of the blood-brother off-limits for marriage. Another important difference is that while natural brotherhood was very hierarchical, with younger brothers expected to deferential to the elder ones, the blood-brotherhood was deliberately egalitarian. Perhaps the most important distinction is shown in Azande sentimental opinion, saying that "a blood-brother is a much better friend than a real brother."[10]

Another well-studied blood-brotherhood tradition is that of the Kaguru of central Tanzania. The rite was known by several names, such as lusale, meaning "cuts," or kukikola umbuya, "taking hold of comradeship," or soga, meaning the "application" of the blood to food in the ritual.[11]

Two men wishing to become blood-brothers would decide on a particular day to perform the rite, and ask neighbors and kinsmen to be present to witness the covenant. A sheep was brought and slaughtered. Most of the meat was cooked and prepared for a feast for all present, but the liver was kept aside after roasting it. Each man cut his own chest near the heart—considered to be the organ of thinking and feeling—and smeared his own blood on one part of the liver. Each man then ate the part of the liver with the other's blood, which was believed to permanently mix the blood of the men's bodies.[12]

The two men then made various promises to each other and declared each other to be kinsmen (wandugu). Others who witnessed the ceremony would also refer to them as kin.[13] The men would also begin referring to the true kin of the other by normal kinship terms, such as "mother", and would continue to do so even after the linking blood-brother died.[14]

However, like the previous example, it is the differences between the Kaguru blood-brotherhood and actual kinship which clarify the full meaning of the relationship. For one man to break his oath to the other was "forbidden"; supernatural ills were thought to follow such a betrayal. To do such an injustice to the other would be to offend his own blood, since the men's blood was in common, which would automatically lead to great misfortune or sickness.[15]

Another distinction is that while natural brotherhood among the Kaguru was shaped by the inequalities of age-ranking, the intention of the lusale rite was equality of the men. For this reason, the Kaguru sometimes say that blood-brothers are like twins.[16] Moreover, the lusale relationship was ideally expected to be free of the conflicts over authority that were common between ordinary kin, and the Kaguru might say that blood-brothers were "closer than kin."[17]

Many other blood-brother rituals in Africa made use of eating the blood upon animal liver. In Kenya, examples occurred among the Kikuyu,[18] Kamba,[19] the Duruma,[20] the Giriama and Sania.[21] Other examples have been among the Zaramo[22] and Gogo[23] of Tanzania, and the Ngata[24] of the Upper Congo region. This is possibly because many early peoples presumed the liver to be a storage organ for blood, or even made of blood, because of its color and blobby similarity to a blood-clot. As blood was thought to be the very life of a creature, the liver could be thought as the primary organ of life, as much as the heart has such associations.[25] (It is interesting to consider the actual English word "liver," as well as the German "Leber," both of which would seem to literally mean "that which lives.") This may explain the hunting tradition of many cultures where the liver, or else both the liver and the heart, are the first things so be eaten after a successful kill.

Another of the better-studied blood-brotherhood traditions of Africa is that of the Ganda people of Uganda. This relationship, called mukago, was once so common that every man had at least two blood-brothers, and sometimes as many as six. It was customary for a young man's first mukago to be found for him by his father, who often picked a son of a friend of his. After this first blood-brother, however, an adult Ganda man was free to choose further mukago for himself. The bond created a general promise of mutual aid.[26]

In the Ganda ritual, the two men sat facing each other upon a bark cloth. A coffee berry was divided up between its two beans, each man taking one in hand. Each then made a cut on his stomach and rubbed the bean in his blood. The men then fed each other the beans directly from their palms.[27] Next each man placed a spear and a knife behind himself, symbolizing a promise of mutual protection. The ceremony concluded with a great feast.[28]

The cuts on the stomach were thought necessary so that each man would see the other's blood.[29] The bloodied bean was thought to somehow remain in the body, and to have the ability to swell up and kill an oath-breaker. If either man were to attempt to cheat this magic by not swallowing the coffee-bean, it was thought that the bean would immediately kill him by swelling up in his mouth.

Like natural brotherhood, neither man could marry female relations of the other, and each man would be addressed by members of his mukago's clan by the same kinship terms used for his mukago. The relationship was even inherited, as people would remember and respect such mukago-bonds created by their ancestors.

However, the relationship was not identical to natural kinship; its obligations were thought to take precedence over all natural relations, and the magical sanctions attached were stronger than any associated with ordinary kin. A man was not to refuse his mukago any needed assistance. A murderer might hide with his mukago, even if the victim was one of the latter's relatives. One man might even surrender himself to die in his blood-brother's place. If two mukago met in war, they would spare each other. One might even secretly inform the other if his village was to be attacked.[30]

These are extreme situations. A more mundane use of a mukago-brother was his role as an advocate to carry out a deceased man's will, especially if his wishes might be different from his clan's desires. The mukago's advocacy had clout; in this respect a mukago-brother was a more useful ally than a wife. A dying man without children might will that his mukago's child become his own heir, or even make the mukago himself into the heir—the deceased man's clan would not oppose this. The blood-brother could support a man against his family. Thus he was thought to be more of a brother than one born of the same mother.[31]

This method of placing cuts at the stomach or navel was somewhat common among African blood-brother ceremonies, as was the use of the paired coffee beans. The two frequently co-occur, especially in eastern Africa. Some examples have been found among the rituals of the Hima[32] and Nyoro[33] peoples of Uganda, and also the Haya of Tanzania.[34]

A blood-brotherhood rite performed among the Lango of central and northern Uganda also made use of the coffee bean. The two men involved were cut near the appendix, and each then smeared blood from his cut onto one of two beans from the same coffee berry. The men then exchanged the bloodied beans and ate them. It was thought that if one were to break the oath, his stomach would swell to the point of bursting, and his relations would die as well. A simpler version was practiced in northwest Lango. Each man's forearm was cut, and the men just touched each other's blood with a fingertip, and licked it off. It was believed that if one of the "brothers" were to become sick or die afterwards, the same would happen to the other.[35]

This example of Lango blood-brotherhood shows an accompanying belief in strongly linked fate between the "brothers," and powerful curse effects. Similar examples from Africa are common. A blood-brotherhood rite of the Kamba people of eastern Kenya, using the consumption of blood on a toasted goat's liver, was so sacred an oath of friendship that an oath-breaker was expected to be punished by the god Engai, who would harm his whole village.[36] Among Dinka of south Sudan, a man who even quarreled seriously enough with a blood-brother to ruin the friendship was expected to die.[37] Among several populations of Madagascar, the judges of the native tribunals once would refrain from forcing one of two blood-brothers to make any confession that would betray the other.[38]

Among the Tiv of Nigeria and Cameroon a form of the blood-brotherhood rite was used to seal pacts between clans. Two old men, each a representative of one of the clans, stood on either side of a large grindstone. Each in turn had his hand cut, bleeding upon the surface of the stone. The blood was then mixed together, along with salt, red palm oil and locust bean powder, and the men then both ate some of the mixture. The Tiv men who formed this pact took extreme care not to harm one another's bodies; if one man were to accidentally nick the other while shaving him, for example, they would immediately trade places, the second man carefully putting an identical cut upon the first.[39]

Among the Chagga of Mt. Kilimanjaro, Mt. Meru, and the Moshi area of Tanzania, blood-brotherhood, or mma, was an affair of state, not allowed to private individuals without the chief's permission. It was often used as a declaration of peace between chieftains, and between a chief and his succeeding son when the former abdicated his position. The obligations of mma took precedence over all other human relationships, with the gods acting as avengers and guarantors of the bond—which is probably why the private blood-brotherhoods were feared by the royal authority.

Nevertheless, illegal private mma occurred often. Chagga men making such pacts would make cuts on a hidden part of the body, instead of on the usual location of the right forearm, or try to make the resulting marks look like accidental scars. Alternatively, they would make use of saliva rituals, which were also called mma and considered equivalent. The men drank saliva mixed with milk or beer, or even simply spat into each other's mouths.

Common uses of private mma include promises to take care of valuable property, such as livestock, or to take care of children once the parent has died. It also could seal a promise to keep secret knowledge of a crime, or of the existence of hidden taxable goods. It also could mean a promise by one mma-brother to give the other advance warning if his village was to be attacked.[40]

A blood-brotherhood ritual involving multiple cuts, known as the ceremony of kassendi, was practiced among the Lunda people, of the Democratic Republic of Congo, Angola and Zambia. As the two men to be united held hands, cuts were made upon the clasped hands, at the pits of their stomachs, on their rights cheeks and on their foreheads. Some of the blood from one man was picked up on a stalk of grass and put into a pot of beer for the second to drink; blood from the second was likewise put into beer for the first. While the men drank the beer, others present beat the ground with clubs, uttering statements that confirmed the oath. The two men were then considered as blood relations, and perpetual friends.[41]

The hospitality between Lunda blood-brothers often included one man giving the other access to his wife.[42] This theme of sharing wives—or at least responsibility for them—was occasionally found among African blood-brother traditions. Blood-brothers among the Haja of Tanzania usually considered themselves to have a right of sexual access to the other's wives.[43] Among the Mbunda people of Angola, blood-brothers considered themselves to hold all property in common, including wives.[44] Among the Tanala of Madagascar, blood-brothers would sometimes agree to have their wives in common.[45]

Another ritual with multiple cuts, and also use of personal weapons, was practiced in the Tabora region of Tanzania. The rite was practiced in the sight of elders, as witnesses. Each man made an incision on the other's arm, belly, and thigh. One man then wiped blood from both men onto some meat or a ball of porridge, which was divided for both men to eat. They also applied some blood directly from one man's wounds to the other's. To create a memento of the ceremony, the men then used the blood to stain their weapons, such as arrows, spears, or clubs with easily stained wooden parts. The ritual concluded with an exchange of gifts.[46]

Each man thus promised to avenge the other if he were murdered, and to take care of the other's widowed wife and orphaned children. In theory, if not in practice, the men's wives were considered to be commonly owned. Also, it was thought that when one man died, the other should ideally "follow him in death," but this was certainly seldom done.[47]

The use of weapons in blood-brotherhood rituals, as in the Tabora and Ganda examples, has been recorded in a great variety of African blood-brotherhood rituals. Among the Duruma of the coast of Kenya, the blood-brotherhood ritual involved the use of a native sword. This was placed on the heads of both men, and was tapped with a knife while oaths of mutual aid were sworn, all before eating a fowl's liver which had been smeared with the men's blood.[48] Similarly, in the rite of the Kikuyu of south-central Kenya, a spear and rifle were crossed over the men's heads, and scraped with a blade during the making of oaths.[49]

In a blood-brotherhood ritual among the Rungu of the west coast of Lake Tanganyika, the two men sat facing each other with their legs interlaced and their feet resting on a bow; stuck in the earth between the string and the bow were placed arrows, spears and a rifle, which remained while the men drank blood mixed with honey.[50] Among the Toro of Uganda, a loaded gun was placed between the men at the start of the ritual, and fired off into the air at the finish.[51] Among the Tanala of Madagascar, the men making a blood-brotherhood ritual grasped a spear during the oath-making phase of the ritual; the spear was held vertically with its point down in a bowl which held several ritual items, such as water, grass, ashes and wild ox dung.[52]

A blood-brother ritual was also practiced by the Kerewe people on Lake Victoria. Two men sat on a mat facing each other, and made cuts on their left pectorals near the heart, and sometimes also at their groins. The blood was put into a small ball of "bwita" food or else some milk, and exchanged and eaten. To finish the ceremony the men left the presence of all witnesses, to sleep side-by-side on a single bed. The rite seems to have created true kinship; it was then impermissible for either man to marry the sisters of the other.[53]

The motif of sleeping side by side in this ritual is also found in a few other versions of blood-brotherhood rites in Africa. In Rwanda, the ceremony ended with the two men lying side by side on a mat, pretending to sleep, to show that they were now inseparably united.[54] Among the Nkole and Nyoro people of Uganda, men making blood-brotherhood slept on the same bed or mat the night before the ceremony.[55]

Among the Maasai of Kenya and northern Tanzania a form of the ritual was used as a statement of friendship both between tribes and between individuals. The two contracting parties each cut their left arm, and dipped some bull's flesh in the blood, and then both ate the flesh. This phase of the ceremony was then closed by a swapping of clothing, which was kept overnight. When the garments were returned in the morning, each man took a drink of milk or pombe beer directly from the other's mouth.[56]

A simple blood-brotherhood rite with mutual cutting was practiced among the Twa people in the region of Lake Kivu in central Africa. Each man made a cut on the other's stomach, scraping up some of the blood on his knife, and then licking the blood off of the blade. Exhortations to keep the oath then followed. Each man was to give any needed assistance the other might ask for, and a magical vengeance was to pursue an oath-breaker. This blood-brotherhood was thought to be a bond greater than natural kinship.[57]

Such mutual cutting is not uncommon in African blood-brother rituals. Some other examples are the ritual of the Sania and Giriama of Kenya,[58] and those of the Zaramo and Sagara peoples of Tanzania.[59]

A traditional blood-brother ritual of Benin—part of the region of western Africa that is the geographic home of the Vodun religion—had many unique elements. The ritual might bind together several men at a time, and was conducted at night in the heart of the forest. The participants had to be entirely naked, removing even the tiniest ornament. All sat directly on the bare earth, in a circle. With a single knife, they cut a complete circle in the earth around themselves. This was done without getting up, so that they had to carefully pass the knife behind their backs, and hand to hand. In the center of the circle was a small pit in the earth, and beside it a drinking bowl made from a skull, which contained water, crushed leaves, and the head of a serpent.

The participants were cut on their left hands, and the blood was sopped up on balls of cotton, which were dropped into the skull. All drank from the skull, and then swore loyalty to each other, and promised disaster to the unfaithful. Many different objects might be brought into the ritual depending on the occupations of the participants, such as weapons or farming tools. The rite was often used by those plotting conspiracies, with aims like robbery, murder, or seizure of power.[60]

Among the Pare people of the Pare Mountains region of Tanzania, a traditional blood brotherhood rite involved a direct sucking of blood from man to man. Each man took a thorn, and scratched the skin on the region of his heart several times, until the blood flowed. Then each man licked up some of the blood of the other, and pledged themselves to eternal friendship. Bystanders chanted songs in the meanwhile.[61]

A very similar ritual occurred in the region of Boyoma Falls. One man sat in a chair, and had a cut made on his chest, and the second man knelt before him to suck at the blood. Then the men

exchanged places. The ritual was finished with the shared smoking of a pipe.[62]

These uses of cuts near the heart are not uncommon. Some
other examples of this method have been recorded among the
Sania of Kenya,[63] the Zaramo of Tanzania,[64] and the Malagasy of
Madagascar.[65]

The method of licking or sucking blood directly from the
wounds, as in the previous examples, has been very widespread
through the populous regions of Africa. In the eastern part of the
continent, some examples have been among the Kamba of Kenya,[66]
and the Shambala[67] and Gogo[68] peoples of Tanzania. In central Africa a few instances have been among the Ila of southern Zambia,[69]
the Babwa,[70] Bangala,[71] and Havu[72] peoples of the D. R. Congo,
and the Banda of the Central African Republic.[73] In western Africa some cases have been found among the Bassa[74] and Ibibio[75]
of Nigeria, the Ejagham of southeast Nigeria and Cameroon,[76] the
Glidyi-Ewe of Togo,[77] and the Talensi of Ghana.[78]

An example of the dramatic curses that might be set against the
betrayers of blood-brotherhood is found in a ritual of the Sumbwa
of central Tanzania. As the men sat facing each other on a straw
carpet, a master of ceremonies cut both men on the right legs, and
moved blood directly from one man's wound to the other's. Then
he made a pronouncement such as:

> If either of you break this brotherhood now established
> between you, may the lion devour him, the serpent
> poison him, bitterness be in his food, his friends desert
> him, his gun burst in his hands and wound him, and
> everything that is bad do wrong to him until death.[79]

Among the Gua-Tumbwe of the south-eastern Congo region,
there was a form of the ritual involving use of *gunpowder*. An incision was made on each of the men's right wrists, and blood was
scraped off of each man and put directly upon the cut of the other.
Then the black gunpowder was rubbed into the cut, leaving be-

hind a kind of *small tattoo mark* as a token of the ceremony. The ritual ended with parties describing the curses that would fall upon those who would break the oath in "word, thought or deed."[80]

Several forms of blood-bother rituals in Africa use such direct insertion of blood from wound to wound. Other examples include the ritual of the Mombasa in Kenya,[81] and the rite in Bambara, Bozo and Dogon peoples in Mali.[82] Among the Nyamwezi of Tanzania, a blood-brotherhood rite involved application of blood mixed with butter into cuts made on the men's left sides, below the ribs.[83] Among many tribes of the Congo region, direct contact of blood in this sort of ritual was done by simply rubbing the wounds together, arm to arm.[84]

The traditional culture of the Kongo people, of northern Angola and the narrow south-east part of the Democratic Republic of Congo, included complex initiation ceremonies for marking the transition of boys into men. These ceremonies involved circumcision. Sometimes, Kongo boys would additionally create a blood-brotherhood at the same time as their initiation. One boy would use a piece of manioc-bread to sop up blood directly from the foreskin, and give it to a select friend, who would reciprocate with the same. This "brotherly food" sealed them as blood-brothers for life, and they were to assist each other in all circumstances.[85]

An unusual version of the rite occurred among the Bemba people of Zambia. Each man actually took a *small sliver of flesh* from the arm of the other, which he ate. They thus swore to aid each other at all times. A further physical expression of this blood-brotherhood was that if one man were to die, the other would bury some of his own hair and nail clippings along with him, wrapping them in leaves.[86]

As all these examples show, the meaning of African blood-brotherhood ranged from closest friendship to political or commercial agreements. Although the participants would consider these affairs to be worth a sense of *sacred* commitment, there was a wide variation in the amount of intimacy implied.

There is some evidence that this factor could affect the choice of what body parts were used to extract the blood. Some explorers noted that chieftains, who would be expected to make many political alliances, had highly scarified forearms; explorers and missionaries in Africa who made peace alliances often had blood taken from the forearms or knees, but seldom more intimate body parts.[87]

One such explorer was Sir Henry Morton Stanley, who conducted much exploration of the interior of Africa in the latter nineteenth century, during which he often made blood-brotherhood oaths as gestures of peace. Once, in the area of Bumba, along the Congo River in the north of the present Democratic Republic of Congo, Stanley made a blood-pact with a local chieftain:

> "Myombi, the chief, was easily persuaded by Yumbila to make blood-brotherhood with me; and for the fiftieth time my poor arm was scarified, (...) A young branch of a palm was cut, twisted, and a knot tied in each end; the knots were dipped in wood ashes, and the seized and held by each of us, while the medicine-man practiced his blood-letting art, and lanced us both, until Myombi winced with pain. After which the knotted branch was severed, and in some incomprehensible manner I had become united forever to my fiftieth brother; to whom I was under the obligation of defending against all foes until death."[88]

For sheer number of blood-brothers, Stanley may have held the record.

AN AFRICAN FOLKTALE

In East Africa, there is a widespread legend about a man who became blood-brothers with various animals. Versions with different details have been told among various peoples. A short version is incorporated into a poem by Y. B. Lubambula,[1] where the story's protagonist is equated with 'Kintu,' the name of both the first human man in Baganda myth, and of the first founding king of the Baganda people. Among the Ankole, a lengthier version fancifully explains why their region has many cattle, and is also used to teach children not to be cruel to animals.[2]

Once there was a man who was a hunter and trapper, who lived a simple life with his wife and his cow. One day, he discovers an anteater in his trap. The anteater speaks to him, asking for his life to be spared, and offering to become blood-brothers with the man, since they may be able to help each other in the future. The man agrees, makes blood-brotherhood with Mr. Anteater, and sends him on his way. On later occasions, the same thing happens with several other creatures: a spider, a fly, a tickbird, a cuckoo, a termite, and a snake. So then the man has seven blood-brothers in all.

One day, the man is returning from hunting, and finds that his wife is missing, as well as his cow. No one he asks in his neighborhood has any idea what has happened. But then Mr. Cuckoo tells him that he saw the men of the sky kidnap them, and take them back to their home above. Mr. Spider then spins a web from the earth to the sky dome, so that the man might try to get them back. He climbs up the web along with Mr. Anteater, who is able to dig a hole through the dome to the land beyond. The sky men are surprised to find a man from the earth in their realm, and are impressed with his cleverness when he explains how he got there. The sky men agree to give him back his wife and cow, but only if he completes certain tasks.

In the first task, there is a great quantity of food which must be eaten by the next morning. It is too much for the man, but Mr. Termite and his many relatives eat it all quickly. Next the man must chop and carry away an enormous amount of lumber. Mr. Termite again helps — or in another version with a giant stone to be cut, the man is helped by the Lightning. In either case, Mr. Snake then allows himself to be used as a rope so the man can bundle and carry the pieces.

The sky men now tell the man he can have his wife and cow, if he can only pick them out. He is shown a huge herd of cattle, and a throng of women in veils. Mr. Fly whispers to the man that he has observed the man and his wife several times in their home, and can pick out the wife easily enough, and then flies to her head. Mr. Tickbird similarly knows the back of the man's cow, and flies right to it. Now the sky men are so impressed with the man's cleverness, they make him a gift of many herds of cattle, and he returns to his home a wealthy man.

The story imaginatively plays with the idea that blood-brotherhood is so powerful a bond that it can create friendship between normally impossible allies. It also demonstrates an important expression of male bonding and friendship, to help one another perform tasks. Complementing each other's talents, the blood-brothers are successful even against the powerful and mysterious and godlike "men of the sky."

THE EAGLE AND THE LIZARD

Practices of blood-brotherhood were once widespread through most of the populated regions of Africa, and mentions of blood-brotherhood customs are made in many African folktales and legends. One tale told among the Kaguru of central Tanzania is all about the proper conduct of blood-brothers.[1] The story is very similar in its style to many of Aesop's fables, having animals that speak and create situations with ethical implications, and ending in a specific moral. Important to an understanding of the story is how breaking blood-brotherhood oaths was utterly forbidden in the Kaguru conception—the exchanged blood would magically cause sickness or death.

Once there were an eagle and a monitor-lizard who loved each other. They decided to form a comradeship, and made an un-breakable vow: "From this moment on we are kin. If one of us has anything the other needs, his comrade needs only to ask, and it will be given. To refuse your comrade is forbidden." They then cut themselves and sprinkled their blood upon a meal that had been prepared for the purpose, and ate it. The custom of such comrades was to visit each other frequently, and bring each other things, and so Eagle and Lizard often did just that.

Lizard had several young sons who were spending a lot of time with their friends learning to shoot arrows at small birds. They began to pester their father to help them get some feathers to make better arrows with. Lizard told them, "That should be easy. My comrade, your father, should be able to help with this, and you'll have your arrows after I return." He then prepared for a journey to Eagle's house, and set off at dawn.

When Lizard arrived he was warmly treated to a meal of many different foods. After this, he said to his friend, "Well, now, I didn't come all this way for nothing. Those boys of yours and mine are growing up, and now they're keeping me awake at night, pestering me about getting some good feathers for their arrows. I remembered that eagle feathers are the best for this sort of thing. So I'll give them the ones you have there. That is why I've come today."

His comrade Eagle replied, "Wait a minute. It's not like I keep food in a storehouse. I go hunting for food over great distances every day. Without the feathers I can't fly. What would we do?"

But Lizard responded, "Hey, now, those needy children of mine are your children as well. Are you forgetting how we ate each other's blood? What's mine is yours and what yours is mine. To refuse me the feathers is forbidden." Hearing this, Eagle agreed, and allowed himself to be plucked bare, and Lizard took the feathers away in a bundle.

Thus for many days Eagle and his family grew very thin with hunger, until his feathers finally began to grow back in.

One day, Eagle's wife came to him and said, "Our children are growing up, and will need their drums made for their dances. I've got a woodworker to make the bodies, but we still need some skins for the drumheads. Why don't you go to that lizard friend of yours and get some?"

Eagle thought and answered, "But...aren't those sort of drums made from monitor-lizard skin? If I took his, wouldn't he just die?"

His wife was angered. "Do you forget how little he cared for us when he wanted the feathers? All because of that oath! What should we care if he would prefer to keep his skin?"

The next day, Eagle went to see Lizard. After dining with him he said, "Well, now, I didn't come all this way for nothing. Those children of yours and mine are growing up, and now they're needing some skins for their drums." Lizard began to tremble with fear. His comrade continued. "As you probably know, monitor-lizard skin is the best for this sort of drum. So I'll give them what you have there. That is why I've come today." Lizard then knew he must either die from losing his skin, or die from breaking his blood-oath. With resignation, he lay down as Eagle flayed him bare, took the skin, and left the rest in the sun to rot.

How you do unto your blood-brother may be how he does unto you.

TRACES FROM THE ANCIENT WORLD

Practices of blood-oaths were widespread in the ancient world. There is not only paleographic evidence from Ancient Egypt, but also evidence from the writings of Greek and Roman historicists and rhetoriticians who concerned themselves with the many peoples and customs of the world which was then known to them. Beyond such blood rites, there were also other customs of brother-making between men.

Some very early evidence of blood-brotherhood is found on an inscribed piece of pottery from Egypt's Ramesside period. The text concerns a draughtsman Menna, and his son, the scribe Peroy. The father is concerned with his son's wayward behavior, admonishing him, "You are (engaged) in the wanderings of the swallow and her young ones. You have reached the Delta on a great journey. You mingled with the 'Amu having eaten bread (mixed) with your blood." The 'Amu were a Semitic people who moved into the area of Egypt from Asia. The blood-rite referred to would have taken place around the middle of the 12th century BCE.[1]

A grisly example of a blood-oath occurring in Greece is discussed by first century BCE historian Diodorus Siculus, in his *Historical Library*. He describes a third century BCE conspiracy headed by Apollodorus, who sought to become dictator. Wishing to secure the allegiance of his men, Apollodorus sacrificed a young man as an offering to the gods, and gave his companions both the vitals to eat and the blood mixed with wine to drink.[2]

A less sinister example of some Greeks involved in a blood-ritual of military allegiance is described by 5th-4th c. BCE writer Xenophon in his *Anabasis*, which recounts the expedition of Persian prince Cyrus against his ruling brother Artaxerxes II. Xenophon recounts an episode when the Hellene forces met up with the Persian forces of Persian commander Ariaeus. The commanders of the Greeks met the Persian leaders in Ariaeus' tent and vowed not to betray each other. They confirmed their oath by spilling the sacrificial blood of a bull, a wolf, a boar, and a ram into the hollow of a shield, and dipping their swords and lances into the blood.[3]

An example of a blood-oath among the Romans is described by first century BCE Roman historian Sallust, in his *Bellum Catilinae*, which discusses the conspiracy of Catiline of 63 BCE. Lucius Sergius Catilina was a Roman who sought to overthrow the Republic. Sallust relates a rumor that Catilina assembled his cohorts in his home, and had them pass around and drink from a goblet containing human blood mixed with wine, while making curses against oath-breakers. Only after doing this did Catilina reveal his exact plans.[4] Sallust does not indicate the origin of the blood, but second and third century CE Church leader and Christian apologist Tertullian believed that the schemers had used their own blood.[5]

A very different sort of bond between men not using blood was a practice of legal brother-making in imperial Rome. Second and third century Roman jurist Julius Paulus is cited in the *Digesta* of the Code of Justinian discussing this legal bond. He describes how one man could properly make another his heir simply by declaring, "Let this man be an heir to me," with the indicated man present. Paulus further states that in this way a man who was not a brother, but loved with brotherly affection, became a properly instituted heir with the description of "brother." [6]

Herodotus, fifth century BCE Greek writer who is often called "the Father of History" mentions blood-oaths in his *Histories*. He mentions that the Lydians (a people of Asia Minor) and the Medes would seal oaths by making cuts on their arms, each party then licking up the blood of the other. [7] Herodotus also describes a blood-oath ritual that was a pledge of friendship among Arabs. A third-party cuts the two men making the pledge on their hands by their thumbs with a sharp stone. He then takes threads from the men's cloaks, and uses it to smear the blood on seven stones that have been placed upon the ground between them. He calls upon the gods as he does this.[8]

Athenaeus of Naucratis, 2nd and 3rd century Greek rhetoritician, mentions a blood-oath of friendship among the people of Carmania (a region corresponding to present-day Kerman province in south-eastern Iran.) He states that in drinking bouts, the Carmani would sometimes open veins in their foreheads, letting the blood flow into their wine, and then drink the mixture. The Carmani thought that this drinking of one another's blood was the highest affirmation of friendship.[9]

Roman senator and historian Publius Cornelius Tacitus, of the first and second centuries CE, leaves evidence of blood-rites among the rulers of lands of the Caucasus region in his *Annales*. He recounts how Iberian prince Rhadamistus once engaged in a ploy to feign interest in a blood-compact of peace with Armenian king Mithridates. Tacitus also describes the form of such a ritual among kings. The two rulers would clasp their hands, and have their thumbs tightly tied together with a knot. After the blood was squeezed into the thumb tips, they were cut, and the two men licked up the blood in turn. Tacitus says this exchange of blood gave the alliance a mystical sanction.[10]

Another example of a blood-oath among the Armenians is related by first century CE writer Valerius Maximus in his *Memorable Doings and Sayings*. One Sariaster, a son of the Armenian king Tigranes, conspired along with several of his friends against his father. The conspirators all cut their right hands, and then sucked the blood in turn.[11]

There is some evidence of blood rites among the Scythian people, who lived on the broad steppe lands north and north-east of the Black and Caspian seas. In his *Histories*, Herodotus describes the manner by which Scyths made oaths. A large earthenware bowl was filled wine, and blood of those making the oath was mixed in. Then a scimitar, arrows, a battle-axe and a javelin were dipped into the blood, while curses were made against oath-breakers. The ritual was concluded with the contractors drinking from the bowl. [12]

Second century CE rhetoritician Lucian of Samosata also refers to a blood-oath of friendship among the Scyths in his *Toxaris*, a work which takes the form of a dialogue about between a Scyth and a Greek about friendship. Toxaris, the Scyth, says that this form of friendship is made only with men who are found to be brave and capable of great deeds, and is pursued with the same patience and seriousness as courting for marriage. The men make a solemn vow to live together and to be ready to die for one another, if need be. The bond is sealed by cutting the fingers and dripping the blood into a cup; the men then dip their sword points into the cup and drink from it simultaneously. Toxaris says further that such compacts may include no more than three men, and that the Scyths compare men with excessive numbers of friends to promiscuous women. [13]

WESTERN AND NORTHERN EUROPE

Traces of blood-brotherhood customs and similar rites in Northern and Western European cultures are found in several of the myths and legends of the region. There are also eye-witness accounts of the practices by a few of Europe's early historians and travelers. Some of the practices survived rather late, sometimes as customs of underground criminal societies.

Blood-brotherhood customs were part of the culture of the heathen Norse, and the practice is mentioned often in Norse sagas. It often was used to form a pact of peace among men who were previously enemies, and also often involved a promise by each man to be the other's avenger. The ritual blood-bond was considered an even stronger tie than natural relations.[1]

A detailed account of the methods of a Norse blood-brotherhood ritual appears in the *Gísla Saga Súrssonar* (Saga of Gisli Sursson), one with four men making a bond simultaneously. The men went out upon a sandy spit of land that jutted out into the sea. They cut up a long strip of the grassy turf, being careful to leave the ends still connected to the ground, so that the strip could be lifted up into an arch. The strip was propped up with a spear that was ornamented with runes. The spear was quite tall; a man reaching up could just touch the rivets attaching the spearhead to the shaft. All four men were to pass under and through the lifted sod. Each man then opened a vein and let the blood drip together into the hollow of earth under the arch, and then they mixed together the blood and soil. Then they fell together to their knees, and calling to the gods as witnesses, swore to treat each other as brothers and to avenge one another. [2]

This form of blood-brotherhood ritual with the blood mixed into the earth is rather unique, and scholars have proposed several different interpretations. The passing under the turf may represent a death and rebirth, as if descending into the dirt of the grave and back; the men were then dead to their previous lives as separate men, but reborn with one life.[3] Another possibility is that the men made each other as brothers by a bloody birth from the common "womb" of the earth. Similarly, the ritual may have meant that the men created a relationship by joining their blood with all of their differing deceased ancestors, conceived as dwelling beneath the earth. The ritual might even have been a kind of trial by ordeal; whether the loop of turf stayed whole or collapsed during the ritual was a sign of whether the intended brotherhood was to be a success.[4]

There is evidence of another blood-rite with blood entering the ground that was practiced among the Danes. Twelfth and thirteenth century Danish historian Saxo Grammaticus ("Saxo the Learned") wrote in his *Danish History* that the ancient Danes, when forming a league, had a custom of sprinkling their footprints with one another's blood. This reciprocal "bartering" of blood sealed a pledge of friendship.[5]

Some blood-brotherhood rites were also practiced among the Germans. At both Helmstädt and Leipzig fraternity initiations among university freshmen once were done by cutting the men's arms, and letting the blood mix in a goblet, which the men then drank while kneeling. Blood-mixing was also involved in an antiquated German superstition. It was thought that if two friends wanted to stay in communication even when separated far from one another, they could mutually cut each other, and let blood drip directly into each other's wounds. Later, whenever one friend stung or pricked himself on the wound, the other should feel it, too; the number of pricks would communicate the message.[6]

Some customs involving blood and names or writing were once tokens of friendship among young German men. In one custom, the men would each use their own blood to write a page in an album kept by the other. In another custom, one man would carve the name of his companion onto his own knotted walking-stick, and then use his own blood to stain the carved letters.[7]

Blood-rites were once often practiced among the Celtic peoples of Scotland and Ireland, and are also referred to in Irish mythology. Blood-brotherhood existed in the Scottish Highlands even as late as the 18th century. Ancient leagues of friendship were sealed by each drinking a drop of blood from the other, usually drawn from the little finger. This bond had a religiously sacred character, and any man who broke such a pact was shunned and deemed an unfit topic of conversation. A similar rite of mutual blood-drinking was practiced among the Irish as confirmation of friendship. Another blood custom that continued late into Irish history was the drinking of the blood of dead relatives, with the purpose of either obtaining their virtues, or else bringing oneself into deeper rapport with them. The same idea is touched on in an old tragic folk-song of the Hebrides, "Ailean Donn," which declares: "I could drink, though to the aversion of others, not of the red wine of Spain, but of the blood of thy body after being drowned." [8]

Thirteenth century Benedictine monk and chronicler Matthaeus Parisiensis wrote in his *Historia Anglorum* of an historical blood-pact which occurred among several Scots, Irish and Manx in 1236. After the death of the Lord Alan of Galloway, the king of the Scots, Alexander II decided that the deceased lord's inheritance should go to his three legitimate daughters, but none to his illegitimate son, Thomas. Hugh de Lacy, a son-in-law of the late Alan, opposed this decision, and he and many others from Galloway, the Isle of Man and parts of Ireland formed a conspiracy of revolt against Alexander, with the aim of restoring the territory of Galloway to Thomas, or his family. To seal their pact, the chiefs of these groups all drew blood from a vein near their hearts, and mixing it together in a large cup, drank to one another from it.

Thus they formed a kindred bond that was unbreakable in either success or failure, even at the risk of their heads.[9]

In the practices of the Age of Chivalry, knights forming a brotherhood in arms sometimes did so by drinking each other's blood.[10] A similar practice is mentioned in Arthurian legend, in the romance of *Lancelot of the Lake*, in a scene where three knights swear companionship by being bled from their right arms and mixing the blood. Some of the blood is sent to a fourth ally who is healed when he is anointed with it.[11]

In early medieval France, there was a fashion for having oneself bled for its alleged medical uses, a practice introduced to French society by an Arabian doctor. People not only had themselves bled when feeling ill, but also in order to mix the blood with that of a friend, as a token of affection and eternal friendship, or else to seal a relationship of brothers in arms. Bertrand du Guesclin, a 14th century Breton knight known as "The Eagle of Brittany" and also once Constable of France, created a brotherhood in arms with soldier Olivier de Clisson, also known as "The Butcher," by mixing their blood in this way.[12] De Clisson joined Du Guesclin on his campaigns against the English during the Hundred Year's War, and took over the role of Constable after Du Guesclin's death.

In Italy, blood-rites were used in the initiation ceremonies of the *Camorra*, a Mafia-like criminal underground society centered in Naples. Different rites were used in initiation of members to different degrees. A novice youth wishing to show his courage and devotion, to become promoted to the lower degree of *picciotto di sgarro* would normally have to disfigure or kill a person selected by the Camorra, but if there were presently no order for any such target to be harmed, the initiation took the form of a modified knife duel between the novice an already received picciotto, the latter chosen by lot. This duel was called the *tirata*, a "drawing" of blood, and was not a lethal duel. The two young men were to strike only at each other's knife-arms, and as soon as the first drop of blood was drawn, both combatants embraced, and the initiation was completed.[13]

A blood-ritual was also involved in the initiation of a picciotto to the higher degree of *Camorrista*, which implied full membership in the band. The initiate and some other members of the society gathered round a table on which lay a dagger, a lancet, a loaded pistol, and a glass of poisoned wine or water. The candidate had one of his veins opened, and dipping his hand into his own blood and holding them out to the others, he swore loyalty to the band, promising to carry out its orders and to keep its secrets. He then stuck the dagger into the table, cocked the pistol, and brought the drinking glass to his lips to show he was ready to die for the organization. The Master of the Camorra then stopped him, and placing his right hand on the head of the kneeling candidate, used his left hand to shatter the glass, empty the pistol into the air, and pull the dagger from the wood, presenting it to the new companion. He then embraced the initiate, as did the others.[14]

Blood-rites more similar to the common forms of blood-brotherhood ritual were used in the initiations of the *Mala Vita*, (literally "Evil Life,") another Italian criminal organization, which was possibly an offshoot of the Camorra. The leader of the band and the novitiate both made wounds in their chests, and then they sucked and drank each other's blood.[15]

THE CATTLE RAID OF COOLEY

The *Táin Bó Cúailnge* (The Cattle-Raid of Cooley) is the one of the central stories of The Ulster Cycle, one four great epic works of Irish mythology. Although written in Christian times, The Ulster Cycle depicts an earlier pagan era. The Táin itself is the story of a war between the Irish lands of Ulster and Connacht, and central to its depiction are two great heroes, Cúchulainn and Ferdiad, who happen to be blood-brothers.

Cúchulainn is the son of the chief Celtic god, Lugh, and the mortal woman Deichtine, the sister of King Conchobor of Ulster. His fighting skills include mastery of the *gae bulga*, an ingenious spear which enters a body as one, but which then opens up into thirty barbs, filling the body cavity so well that it cannot be removed without killing the victim. In the greatest heat of battle, Cúchulainn undergoes the "Warp-Spasm," a berserk battle-madness which so distorts his body that he hardly appears human. Ferdiad is also a great warrior, and possesses the *conganchness*, an unusual armor which is very strong, but slight enough that it fits him as a horny second skin. The two men were nursed and trained together by the warrior-queen Scathach in their youth, and it was she who encouraged them to become blood-brothers in a blood-drinking ceremony.

The events of the *Táin* begin with a comical bit of nighttime "pillow-talk" between Queen Medb and King Ailill of Connacht. They argue over which of them is the wealthier. Medb believes that Ailill is the one who has materially gained the most from their marriage, and wants him to admit it, but he replies that he has one valuable item that she does not—the White Bull of Connacht. There is only one like it, the Dun Bull of Cooley, possessed by Ulster. These are no ordinary cattle; they are both perfectly intelligent creatures and have previously lived in the forms of birds, stags, fish, dragons, worms, and originally, two men of the fairy-folk. Ailill has won the argument, but now Medb begins to scheme to even the score by gaining the Dun Bull of Cooley for herself. After attempts to buy it fail, Medb makes recourse to invasion.

The timing of this is terrible for Ulster, as most of its men are then under the effect of the *cess*, a curse which periodically sickens and weakens them to the point of being unable to fight. Only Cúchulainn is in any condition to defend the realm. He successfully invokes the right of single-combat, and so takes up position at a ford in a river at the edge of Ulster territory, where Connacht's champions must meet him one by one. Cúchulainn subdues dozens of foes over a period of months. Eventually, Medb and her advisers turn their attentions to one warrior who just might be a match to Cúchulainn, if he will agree to aid them— Ferdiad.

Ferdiad meets Medb and her advisers at her camp. She plies him amply with drink, and makes him several offers. She will give him rich treasures, part of her kingdom's land, and even the hand of her daughter Finnabair, if he will challenge Ulster's champion. But Ferdiad is not willing to do to battle against his childhood friend and blood-brother, and refuses each time. Medb then slyly says to her advisers, "So perhaps what Cúchulainn says is true..." Ferdiad asks what, and she answers that Cúchulainn says Ferdiad has lost his courage, and wouldn't be too hard to defeat. This is pure fabrication on Medb's part, but Ferdiad believes it, and in his anger swears to fight Cúchulainn for Connacht.

The camps of the two warriors are set up on opposite sides of the river. Ferdiad and Cúchulainn meet at the ford, and greet each other with harsh words, renouncing their friendship. On this first day of battle, they choose to fight with light spears and darts. No missile thrown is a miss, but both men's defense is as good as his offence, and so no blood is drawn. At noon, they switch to heavier spears and now both draw blood. The battle is temporarily halted at evening. Cúchulainn and Ferdiad then run to each other and embrace and kiss. After each retires to his camp, Cúchulainn sends to Ferdiad half of the healing herbs and curing charms he has, and Ferdiad sends to Cúchulainn half of his food and drink.

On the second day of battle, the two men choose to fight with broad-blade lances, using their horses and chariots. This time they wounds they deliver each other are so great, that birds might have flown through the gaps, picking out bits of blood and flesh. Yet at the end of this day's fighting, they exchange the same kisses and gifts.

The third day of battle is yet the more terrible. Cúchulainn ruefully declares, "Alas, O Ferdiad, a pity it is for thee to oppose thy foster-brother and thy comrade and friend, on the counsel of any woman in the world!"[1] They choose to fight with heavy swords, and the lumps of flesh they cut off one another are as large as the head of a month-old child. When they cease fighting that evening, they are cold to each other, and share no more the gifts and kisses.

The fourth day is the decisive test. They choose to fight by "the Feat of the Ford" — all weapons allowed. The Warp-Spasm comes over Cúchulainn, making his form monstrous. They fight all day, with such vigor that the water is thrown out of the ford, leaving the riverbed dry between them. Cúchulainn then chooses to deploy the *gae bulga*, and seeing the best way to get it past Ferdiad's armor, he uses his foot to launch it upward into Ferdiad's body. Ferdiad's death is now certain. Cúchulainn quickly rushes to him and picks him up, and carries him as he runs to the north shore of the river, so that his blood-brother will die on the land of Ulster, and not on the land of the enemy. Cúchulainn cries out a poetic lament, which includes the following stanzas:

Then our famous nurse made fast
Our blood-pact of amity,
That our angers should not rise
'Mongst the tribes of noble Elg!

Sad the morn, a day in March,
Which struck down weak Daman's son.
Woe is me, the friend is fall'n
Whom I pledged in red blood's draught![2]

Cúchulainn goes on to fight many other men after this. In the meantime, the Dun Bull of Cooley has itself been fighting with the White Bull of Connacht and has defeated it. But as it returns home to Ulster at the end of the *Táin*, it dies of sheer exhaustion. All the bloodshed and death has been in vain.

Here the *Táin* ends, but further parts of *The Ulster Cycle* depict the final deaths of both Cúchulainn and Medb. The paradoxical behavior of Cúchulainn and Ferdiad during the days of battle dramatizes simultaneously both the courageous ferocity of the ideal warrior, and the strong emotional attachment that blood-brothers may have with each other. Cúchulainn's chiding of Ferdiad for trusting Medb's counsel suggests that the male bond should ideally guard itself against threatening outside influences, especially feminine ones. Significantly, it is the idea that Cúchulainn has been *disrespecting* him that turns him against his blood-brother. The final action of the battle days, with Cúchulainn rushing the dying Ferdiad across the river, has been frequently been portrayed in the Irish arts. In County Louth there is a statue depicting the moment.

ODIN AND LOKI

Blood-brotherhood is a theme in Norse mythology and legend, both in the representation of the pre-Christian gods of the Norse and Germanic peoples who are depicted in the Eddas, as well as among the legendary ancestors and heroes whose stories are told in the elaborate Norse sagas. It happens that a blood-brotherhood exists between two of the mythology's principle gods, Odin and Loki.

Known by such epithets as "All-Father" and "Greybeard," Odin is the chieftain of the Norse Gods, the Aesir. He is a creator of the earth and humanity. He is concerned with the Ragnarök or "the fate of the Gods," an impending battle between the Aesir and their foes, the giants, who will destroy both the earth and the home of the gods themselves, but will spare just a few gods and one man and one woman to begin things anew. Using his battle-maids, the Valkyries, Odin often causes brave men to die in battle, taking their souls to Valhalla, the "Hall of the Slain," where they will practice for the Ragnarök. Odin is thus a god of battle and death, but he also is a god of magic and wisdom, as he constantly seeks to learn magical secrets to aid his ends, like a wizard in development.

Loki is a very different sort of god, possibly descended from the Giants. He is a trickster, with a power to change his form, and a habit of changing his ways and loyalties. He is cunning and clever, often helping ingeniously to solve the Aesirs' problems, sometimes problems he has caused himself. In the mythology as presented in the Eddas he begins as an uncertain ally of the Aesir, but gradually turns into their archfiend. It is Loki who sets of the course toward the Ragnarök, by causing the death of Odin's son, Balder. It seems ironic that these two gods should be blood-brothers, but it is part of the plot of the Lokasenna, one of the shorter myths in the Poetic Eddas.

The story begins not long after the killing of Balder. The Gods have assembled at the Hall of Aegir for a great feast. Loki shows up at the hall, and his presence brings a hush of quiet to the crowd. Bragi, the god of poetry, warns Loki that his company isn't wanted, but Loki speaks to Odin, pressing upon his blood-brotherhood:

> Art mindful Óthinn,
>   how in olden days we
> blended our blood together?
>
> Thou said'st that not ever
>   thou ale would'st drink
> but that to us both were borne.[1]

Desiring to keep the peace, Odin somewhat reluctantly makes room for Loki at the table. But soon Loki draws the gods into a protracted insult contest. He calls Bragi the most cowardly of gods, says Odin has a past of "womanly ways," says that Freya, the goddess of fertility, has slept with all the gods in the hall, and accuses the sea-god Njord of sleeping with his own sister. The rancor doesn't end until Thor threatens to shut Loki up with his hammer. Loki then leaves, uttering a curse that the hall and its owner, Aegir, will be destroyed in flames. Presumably, at the Ragnarök, this comes true.

The overall tone of the myth is more comical than devotional, but it dramatizes the serious matter of the completion of Loki's transformation into the Aesir's enemy. That a blood-brotherhood exists between the mythology's two primary actors shows how well-known the concept of blood-brotherhoood was to the pagan Germanic peoples. It could be said that with Loki as the cause of the Ragnarök, the whole of the Norse mythology is an elaborate story of a broken blood-brotherhood.

THE VÖLSUNGA SAGA

Written by an unknown Icelandic author in the thirteenth century, the Völsunga Saga, (Saga of the Volsungs), is the greatest of the epic myths of the early Scandinavian peoples, and certainly the most famous. The work was based primarily on a poetic version of the Norse myths, The Poetic Edda, as well as orally transmitted folk myths. It shares much content with the medieval German Niebelungenlied, (Song of the Niebelungs). The Völsunga Saga was the primary source of the themes of Richard Wagner's opera cycle, Der Ring des Nibelungen, (The Ring of the Nibelung), and more loosely inspired J.R.R. Tolkien's epic fantasy, The Lord of the Rings. It has even inspired plots of science fiction, such as Melvin Burgess' novel Bloodtide. Blood-brotherhood (as well as other effects of blood) is critical to the deeds and fate of the central hero, Sigurd.

Sigurd, (or Siegfried in the German version) is of the family of the Volsungs and thus a descendant of Odin. He possesses a mighty sword, Gram, which was originally from Odin, and once was broken, but which Sigurd has reforged. With this sword he has slain the dragon Fafnir. Among the treasures he wins from the dragon's horde is a "helm of terror," and a golden ring, Andvaranaut, (Ring of Andvari) which bears a curse, unknown to Sigurd: it will bring the destruction of all who own it. Sigurd tasted a drop of blood from the dragon's heart, and thus gained the power to understand the speech of birds. (In the German version of the myth, the *Niebelungenlied*, he bathes in its blood, and develops an armored skin like the dragon's scales.)

It is by overhearing birds' conversation that Sigurd learns about the maiden Brynhild. Beautiful and wise, she was once a Valkyrie, one of Odin's battle-maids, a minor deity charged with the task of choosing which brave heroes would die in battle, to be taken to Valhalla. Brynhild once disobeyed Odin's command about which warrior to take, and thus lost her immortality. Odin then placed her in a stone hall in the mountains, which was ringed by a wall of fire. There she lay unconscious, pricked by a thorn from the Tree of Sleep.

Searching the mountains, Sigurd finds the hall, and successfully dares to ride through the flames. After waking Brynhild, the now-mortal maiden explains that she has vowed to marry only the most brave and fearless man; the wall of flame was a test. Sigurd agrees to wed her sometime in the future, and seals the vow by giving her the cursed ring.

Sigurd is later welcomed at the hall of King Gjuki (of the family of the Niebelung in the German version of the myth). He is soon held in great favor there, and becomes great friends with the king's two sons, Gunnar and Högni, but less so with the half-brother, Guttorm. The queen, Grimhild, is very impressed with Sigurd and wishes that he would marry her daughter, Gudrun. Grimhild connives to slip Sigurd a magic drink of Forgetfulness, and he loses memory of Brynhild altogether. He then becomes warm to Gudrun, and marries her. He further seals his bond with the family by becoming blood-brothers with both Gunnar and Högni.

Queen Grimhild then persuades Gunnar to try to win Brynhild for his own wife. The blood-brothers Gunnar and Sigurd ride off to the mountain hall, but Gunnar is unable to ride through the flames. However, the two have learned a bit of magic from Grimhild; they exchange their outward forms, and thus Sigurd rides through to the hall in Gunnar's guise. Brynhild is quite surprised, not expecting to receive a second suitor who is at least as brave as the first, but because of her vow she agrees to wed the seeming-Gunnar. He gives her another ring, and takes the Andvaranaut from her.

This complex situation does not make the household of King Gjuki the happiest one. Brynhild is haughty toward Gudrun, wife of the fickle Sigurd. One day the two women come to argue about which of them has the nobler husband. Gudrun rather unwisely reveals all she knows about Sigurd's shape-shifting and Gunnar's complicity, and shows Brynhild the proof—the Andvaranaut ring is now on Gudrun's hand.

Brynhild is incensed. She has not married the bravest man the world, but has only been tricked by him. She does not accept Sigurd's apology, nor listen to his defense that he was under a strange spell of forgetfulness when he acted. She urges Gunnar to kill Sigurd, if he would keep her love. Gunnar and Högni are then in a dilemma, as they want to save Gunnar's marriage, but do not want to break their vow of blood-brotherhood with Sigurd. They connive that it would be well enough if Sigurd's slaying were not done by their own hands, and convince their half-brother Guttorm to do the deed, by maddening him with a magical dish of snake and wolf flesh. He runs Sigurd through with a sword as he sleeps, but Sigurd lives long enough to slay Guttorm in return. Brynhild cannot be made any happier yet regardless; she rues the killing, even though it was she who conceived it. As she laments in *The Poetic Edda*:

> Forgettest, Gunnar,
> > altogether how your blood ye
> both did blend under sward?
>
> Him now hast thou
> > with hate requited, and foully felled,
> who foremost made thee [1]

Finally, at Sigurd's funeral, Brynhild throws herself upon the cremation flames.

THE FÓSTBRAEÐRA SAGA

Instances of blood-brother rituals and relationships appear often in Norse mythology and in the Norse sagas. There is even a Blood-Brothers Saga. Written in the thirteenth century, the Fóstbraeðra Saga is concerned with the lives of two young braves, Thormód and Thorgeir. The two grow up together in the Isafjord region of Iceland, and finding themselves to be of similar character, they become great friends. They swear an oath of brotherhood, including a promise that either would avenge the other's death, and so they go "under three strips of sod"1—referring to the Norse blood-brotherhood ritual where turf is raised into an arch and blood mixed into the earth.

The two prove to make a ferocious combination, stirring up enough trouble that they become unpopular and feared. There are some important differences of personality between them. Thormód is the more contemplative one, and something of a ladies' man. He is also a poet, and many episodes in the saga are concluded with verses attributed to him, forty stanzas in all. These verses often praise the exploits of Thorgeir, an effective killer.

Thorgeir first draws blood when he avenges the death of his father at the hands of Jod, an experienced fighter and chieftain. Thorgeir travels to Jod's home and spears him. As Thorgeir is only fifteen, people are amazed. Sometime later, the two sworn brothers are staying at the home of the widow Sigurfjold. The blood-brothers discuss some whaling plans, but the widow suggests that they try for a "braver and better catch"—two local troublemakers and thieves, Ingolf and Thorbrand. The blood-brothers confront these two, saying the men must give up either their ill-gotten property, or their lives. When Thorbrand says that the young Thorgeir would surely meet his own death, Thorgeir responds, "Like others in my family, I can prophesy by my dreams. I have dreamt a great deal about myself, but very little about you."[2] Thorgeir and Thormód slay their foes, and their fearsome reputation increases. There are more battles, including one where Thorgeir kills a man over possession of a whale, an act for which he is declared an outlaw.

It comes to pass that Thormód and Thorgeir have a falling-out. The prose text and the included poem tell different stories as to why. According to the prose, Thorgeir relates that the two blood-brothers are probably the most feared men in Iceland, and goes on to ask which of the two of them would be able to defeat the other. Thormód responds that Thorgeir shouldn't be talking or thinking about such a thing, and quits their friendship. The poem that accompanies the chapter, however, states that people who begrudged the might of the blood-brothers spread rumors and slander to break them up.

The two go separate ways. Thorgeir is able to have his outlaw status removed, and becomes one of the guardsmen of Norwegian King Olaf. Thorgeir frequently travels between Iceland and Norway in this capacity, and commits several more slayings. Thormód's life takes a less exciting turn. He is frequently bored at the home of his family. He begins simultaneous romantic affairs with two different women. One is Thorbjörg, known also as "Coal-Brow," for whom Thormód writes a lengthy love poem. When the other woman Thordís hears about this, and is jealous, Thormód recites her the same verse with a few changes, to make it be about her. This phase of Thormód's life, concerned mainly with romantic affairs with women, ends suddenly when he learns of Thorgeir's death.

In Iceland, Thorgeir has been slain by Thorgrím, "the Troll," a chieftain from the Greenland colony, and his assistant, Thórarin, known as "Arrogance." Thorgeir managed to kill fourteen of his foes before he fell. Insultingly, Thórarin Arrogance made a trophy of Thorgeir's head, which he carried with him from place to place before he was himself killed. Thorgrím Troll has gone back to Greenland.

Thormód then enters King Olaf's guard himself, by which he is able to get passage to Greenland. He arrives there during a General Assembly, where many booths are assembled. His task could be difficult with so many people being near his target. In fact, a large crowd is gathered at the booth of Thorgrím Troll, who entertains them all with a great battle story—about Thorgeir. The start of rain drives the crowd away, but Thormód keeps Thorgrím Troll outside a little while with questions about the story he was telling and suddenly deals him a lethal blow to the head with a hatchet. Hiding the hatchet in his robe, Thormód then sits down with Thorgrím's head arranged on his lap and cries out that the man has been hurt. After people come to see, he tells some to look for the perpetrator, and while the others are distracted with tending to Thorgrím, Thormód slips away in the general confusion.

Thormód cannot return home to Iceland immediately, and must hide in a cave to be safe from Thorgrím Troll's allies until his own friends are able to arrange for him to sail back. The remainder of the saga tells about Thormód's continuing service to King Olaf, and his death defending his king in battle.

The saga is not always clear about its characters' motivations. There is uncertainty as to the actual cause of the sworn-brothers' break-up. The episode could suggest a lesson that blood-brothers must always respect one another—or it could be a warning about splitting over petty bickering. Thormód's exact reason for his journey to Greenland is also ambiguous. He may be doing his best to reconcile the broken friendship, insofar as he could with one friend already dead. He may see the blood-sworn promise of vengeance as a duty going above and beyond the ordinary duties of the eliminated friendship. Either way, the saga is an example of how blood-brotherhood can inspire acts of great courage and determination by one brother on behalf of the other.

DIE GÖTTERDÄMMERUNG

Wilhelm Richard Wagner was a 19th century German composer and conductor, known primarily for his operas. His most famous operatic work is *Der Ring des Nibelungen* (*The Ring of the Nibelung*), a cycle of four operas, based upon both German and Norse mythology. Wagner paid particular attention to the blood-brotherhood motif of the Norse *Völsunga Saga* in the fourth opera of his *Ring* cycle, *Die Götterdämmerung* (Twilight of the Gods), where the very language of the scene is a script of a blood-brother ritual. There are small variances with the version of events in the *Völsunga Saga*; the names of the three men are Siegfried, Gunther, and Hagen, as in the German *Niebelungenlied*. Also, in Wagner's version, only Siegfried and Gunther become blood-brothers, instead of all three. Hagen aids them in the ceremony, destroying the drinking-horn afterwards, probably as a safeguard against anyone else drinking from the now tainted cup and inadvertently getting mixed up in the blood-magic. The form of ritual, though ancient Norse aren't known to have practiced the drinking of blood, is very similar to a blood-rite once practiced in Germany. [1]

The German language in this scene (as in most of Wagner's work) is dense with repetition of sounds, adding to the ritual effect. The English translation here deliberately uses antiquated and somewhat barbarous English, to allow a version that matches the poetic style of the original text, whilst keeping quite close to its sense. [2]

GUNTHER

Let us swear an oath!

SIEGFRIED

Blood-brotherhood we'll swear!

Hagen fills a drinking-horn with fresh wine, and holds it out to Sieg-fried and Gunther. These two cut their arms with their swords and then hold them over the opening of the horn for a short time.

Siegfried and Gunther lay two of their fingers upon the horn, which Hagen meanwhile holds between them.

SIEGFRIED

Blooming life's
bracing blood
I have dripped in the drink.

GUNTHER

Brother-fervid,
boldly blended,
our blood in the drink will bloom.

BOTH

My troth I drink to my friend.
Fine and free
bloom from the bond,
blood-brotherhood today!

GUNTHER

Breaks a brother the bond...

SIEGFRIED

Betrays a friend the troth...

BOTH

What drank we dearly
this day in droplets
will spout out in streams;
vengeance for the friend!

GUNTHER

He drinks and hands the horn to Siegfried.

So bid I the bond.

SIEGFRIED

So drink I the troth.

He drinks and hands the emptied drinking-horn to Hagen, who strikes it into two pieces with his sword. Siegfried and Gunther clasp each other's hands.

The "conditional curse" expressed in the end is not known to be a part of the Norse custom, but the idea exists in blood-brotherhood traditions from Africa to Borneo; the blood itself will avenge the betrayed. Slightly different from the Norse myth, Wagner's version of the story places this scene right after Siegfried and Gunther have decided to collude to win the hand of Brynhild for Gunther. This makes it an example of the idea of blood-brotherhood being formed between men on a mission; the male-bond can be formed between men who share aggression against a common target.

CHAUCER: THE KNIGHT'S TALE

Geoffrey Chaucer, fifteenth century English author and poet, is often thought of as the "father" of English literature, having been among the first to work in contemporary English in an era when most serious literature was in Latin or French. His most famous work is The Canterbury Tales, a collection of stories within a general story. A company of travelers, of many different professions, are journeying together on a pilgrimage to a shrine in Canterbury Cathedral. To pass the time, they hold a contest to see who can tell the best tale. Several of these tales happen to involve "sworn brothers," a phrase thought by some scholars to signify the Medieval English manifestation of the cross-cultural tradition of blood-brotherhood.1 One of these tales, The Knight's Tale, is among the most famous of the work.

The first in *The Canterbury Tales*, *The Knight's Tale* is based on Boccaccio's *Teseida delle nozze di Emilia*.[2] It was a source for the later play, *The Two Noble Kinsmen*, co-written by William Shakespeare and John Fletcher. Pagan in nature, the story is set in ancient Greece, with the Olympian Gods taking part in shaping the course of events. While the story describes no ritual, for cultural appropriateness, the sworn-brotherhood central to the tale ought to be of the blood-drinking sort that was typical to Greece.

Palamon and Arcite are two young men of the royal family of Thebes, and are cousins, yet sworn-brothers as well. When Duke Theseus of Athens sieges and conquers Thebes, the two sworn-brothers are captured and imprisoned in a tower in Athens for many years. One day Emelye, the sister-in law of Theseus, is in a garden by the tower, and Palamon happens to see her through the window. He is immediately struck by love, crying out in pain. He is unsure whether or not he is really seeing the love goddess, Venus, and so he falls on his knees in prayer. Arcite, wondering what all this is about, also looks out at Emelye, and is stricken by sudden love as well, vowing to have her. This would create a rivalry between the two cousins, and Palamon chides his sworn-brother:

> "It nere," quod he, "to thee no greet honour
> For to be fals, ne for to be traitour
> To me, that am thy cosyn and thy brother
> Ysworn ful depe, and ech of us til oother,
> That nevere, for to dyen in the peyne,
> Til that the deeth departe shal us tweyne,
> Neither of us in love to hyndre oother,
> Ne in noon oother cas, my leeve brother,
> But that thou sholdest trewely forthren me
> In every cas, as I shal forthren thee–
> This was thyn ooth, and myn also, certeyn;

> *(lines 1129-1139)*

The lines are a definition of the duties of sworn-brotherhood.

Arcite has his counter-arguments. Love cannot be restrained by any law. Moreover, Palamon's first sight of Emelye counts for little if he didn't realize she was a human woman.

The two cousins are not confined together in their rivalry for long. An ally of Arcite wins his release from the prison, with a condition that he must leave Athens. Wishing to be close to Emelye, he manages to enter the duke's service incognito, gradually rising to the status of a squire. Palamon also escapes several years later. The two rivals happen to meet in a nearby wood, and agree to have a formal duel.

It is as they are fighting that duke Theseus, his wife Ypolita, and Emelye happen to enter the same wood as they are pursuing a stag. The Duke demands to know what this duel is about, and hearing their explanation, wishes to put them both to death. But Emelye and Ypolita are moved to pity seeing the men's wounds, and plead mercy for them. The duke then decides not to execute them, and to let the matter be decided by a dangerous contest instead. A vast tournament is to be held in a year's time, one where the victory will be given to the man who either slays his opponent, or drives him from the lists. The two cousins are to bring a hundred knights each, and the winner will get Emelye's hand.

A great arena is built, with a radius of a mile, and room for thousands of spectators. The structure contains temples for three gods, Venus, Diana, and Mars. Before the battle is to take place, Palamon prays to Venus at the temple, asking that he be able to claim Emelye. He does not care whether it is by winning the battle or otherwise. He receives a sign: the statue of Venus trembles. Emelye also prays at the temple of Diana, asking first that the two sworn-brothers should have peace between them, but if that is not to be, that she should have the one of the two who loves her more. Diana then appears to her, saying that one of the men will be her husband, but does not say which. Arcite prays to Mars, asking that the god aid him in battle. As a sign, the earth trembles, and a voice cries out, "Victory!" These signs would seem hard to reconcile; the story explains that the gods are arguing over what the fate of the mortals should be. The God Saturn says that he has a plan that will meet all the gods' wishes.

On the day of the contest, the duke announces a change in the rules: no killing shall be done. Thus when Arcite first cuts Palamon with his sword, the latter is immediately carried away to the place for the losers to wait. Arcite rides about the arena in victory. Then comes Saturn's surprise, when Pluto shakes the ground with a "furie infernal." Arcite's horse is frightened and throws him off, and his chest is injured as he lands on his saddle-bow. His wounds become infected, and it becomes clear that he will die. He then repents his rivalry with Palamon, and recommends him to Emelye.

Some years later, after the mourning for the dead Arcite is done, Theseus gives away Emelye to Palamon in marriage. They live together in bliss, richness, and health.

The theme of a sworn brotherhood strained by romantic rivalries is common to legends about such male companions. To Chaucer's medieval audience, the detail of him initially mistaking Emelye for a divine being would be a hint of which of the cousins was to be seen as in the right. Appropriately, the connivance of the gods ultimately supports Palamon's views. Not only was Palamon's love the truest, but Chaucer illuminates the moral principle that sworn brothers must never hinder each other, yet only "further" each other in every circumstance.

CHAUCER: THE PARDONER'S TALE

Based on an old legend with several versions, and origins as far back as a Buddhist tale from sometime between 400 to 250 BCE,[1] *The Pardoner's Tale* is the most enigmatic of the stories in Chaucer's *Canterbury Tales*. It is also among the more renown of the tales, having inspired works by other writers of fiction, including J. K. Rowling. The story involves three men who become "sworn-brothers." The teller of the tale, the Pardoner, is a traveling preacher who sells forgiveness for sins, and holy relics. He is strangely open to the other travelers that he is completely hypocritical in this matter, caring nothing for his audiences' souls; he does his trade solely for profit. It is thus ironic that the Pardoner's favorite theme for sermons is *Radix Malorum est Cupiditas,* "greed is the root of all evil," which is also a theme of his tale.

In Flanders there are three young men who are "riotoures," men who live a wild, hedonistic life, given to drinking, gambling and whoring. They have a "blasphemous" habit of swearing oaths on various parts of Christ's body, which the Pardoner depicts as a violent tearing of Christ to pieces. The three men are already drinking one morning in a tavern when they hear a funeral procession pass. The serving boy tells them that the deceased is a friend of the three, who has been killed by a thief known as Death. In fact, he adds, Death has been killing any number of people during a current pestilence. The taverner tells them all how Death has killed every last person in a nearby village. Both speak of Death as a supernormal person. The three rioters are angered and not intimidated, and swear brotherhood as they hatch a plan:

"Ye, Goddes armes!" quod this riotour,
"Is it swich peril with hym for to meete?
I shal hym seke by wey and eek by strete,
I make avow to Goddes digne bones!
Herkneth, felawes, we thre been al ones;
Lat ech of us holde up his hand til oother,
And ech of us bicomen otheres brother,
And we wol sleen this false traytour Deeth.
He shal be slayn, he that so manye sleeth,
By Goddes dignitee, er it be nyght!"
Togidres han thise thre hir trouthes plight
To lyve and dyen ech of hem for oother,
As though he were his owene ybore brother.
And up they stirte, al dronken in this rage,
And forth they goon towardes that village
Of which the taverner hadde spoke biforn.
And many a grisly ooth thanne han they sworn,
And Cristes blessed body they torente —
Deeth shal be deed, if that they may hym hente!

(lines 692-710)

Death will be dead, if only they can catch him! With such great ambition the three set off. They soon find a mysterious old man, who is wrapped up in cloth, except for his face. He looks so strangely ancient, that one of the men asks him how he even keeps living. The old man replies that no-one will take his life, not even Death, even though the old man would wish it. One of the sworn-brothers suspects that the old man is really in alliance with Death as a spy, and threateningly demands that the old man tell them Death's whereabouts. The old man then tells them of an oak tree up a road, where they will find Death.

The three men go to the tree, where they find a great store of gold florins. They are distracted from their original mission. Not wanting to be seen carrying such treasure through the town by day, they choose one man to go fetch food and drink for them all as they will guard the treasure until nightfall. As he is gone on his errand, the other two hatch a treacherous scheme against him to gain his third of the booty: one will play at wrestling him for fun, and the other will stab him as he's held. While they are agreeing to do this, the third man has gotten poison to put into two of the three bottles of wine he has just bought. After he meets them back at the oak tree, he is killed by them just as they planned, and next they are killed by the wine. The old man's statement has come true; at the tree, they do "find Death."

Here, the immorality of avarice leads to self-destruction. That the mechanism of this destruction is also the breaking of a sworn-brotherhood underscores of the moral importance of the bond. Another idea is hinted at⊙we must wonder whether if the three had been good enough to remain loyal, they might have succeeded in their grand quest. The image of death as an anthropomorphic being was a common idea in the medieval era, possibly influenced by the Old Testament image of the "Angel of Death" as a discrete entity. The male bond strengthens aggression against foes outside of itself. In this tale, blood-brothers are willing to vie against the gods, but the disintegration of that bond ruins their mission.

THE OUTLAWS OF INGLEWOOD FOREST

Medieval English ballads were popular forms of verse, performed to music, and often telling romantic tales of heroes. One such English ballad tells the legend of a trio of sworn-brothers, who live as outlaws in the archaic Inglewood forest, an area of both woods and farmlands in northern England that had once been claimed by the royal powers as their own possession. The legend has been in circulation since at least the early fifteenth century. It was one of the many ballads collected by nineteenth century folklorist Francis James Child in his multi-volume work *The English and Scottish Popular Ballads.*[1]

Once there were three yeomen, keen archers, who hunted deer in England's green northern forests. These three men were called Adam Bell, Clim of the Clough, and William of Cloudsley. The three had been made into outlaws for taking venison from the lands of the king. They swore themselves brethren one day, and hid within the Inglewood forest, dwelling there beneath the greenwood trees.

Adam and Clim were single, but William had a wife and children in the city of Carlise, and after being separated from them for over half a year, he became anxious to see them again. He told his two sworn-brothers that he would make the dangerous journey to the city, and that if he did not return the next day, they should consider him imprisoned or dead.

Cloudsley's wife Alice and their three children were overjoyed to see the father of the family again. But an old woman whom they had charitably taken into their home sneaked away to inform the Justice of William's secret return.

The Justice and the Sheriff came with a great rout of men and surrounded William's house. William took his wife and children into the most defensible room of the home, bringing his sword and his bow. Alice herself took up a poleaxe, ready to join the fight. William began shooting at his enemies from the window.

The Sheriff and the Justice ordered the house to be burned. William let his wife and children down from a back window with ropes made of sheets, telling the crowd to work their wreckage on him alone. He continued to fight by himself, but soon the flames were so high that he couldn't aim his arrow out of the window without the fire burning the bowstring. He thought to himself then that it would be a coward's death to burn up with the house, when he could at least run his naked sword through the crowd of enemies.

He left the house and charged with his sword and his buckler, cutting down many men. He fought so fiercely that none could face him alone. The crowd gathered up some wooden planks from doors and windows and together they encircled him, pressing in until he was captured. William was bound hand and foot, and thrown into a dungeon. The Sheriff of Carlisle then declared that William would be executed in the morning, and ordered a gallows to be built. He also ordered the gates of the city walls be opened to no one until the execution was completed.

A little boy who often tended swine for William and Alice heard of this, and knew of a very small crevice in the wall just large enough for him to pass through. He made his way out to Inglewood forest, and told the other two of the sworn-brothers what was to take place in the morning.

Adam Bell and Clim of the Clough then traveled to Carlisle, arrived early in the morning, and found the city gates closed to them. Adam suggested that they pretend to be messengers from the king, and took out a neatly written letter with a seal, reasoning that the porter of the gate might be "no clerke." Indeed, the porter hardly knew how to tell one written word from another, and hastily let in the seeming royal envoys. As soon as they were inside, Adam and Clim wrung the porter's neck, and stole the gate keys from him.

They went with their yew bows to the market place in the center of the city, where they saw a crowd gathered around a gallows. William of Cloudsley was bound hand and foot in a cart, a rope already around his neck. As William lay there the Justice was measuring him for his grave. William said that greater marvels have happened, than the one who measures him for a grave will lie it in himself. The Justice replied that William should have no fear of that, for the Justice will hang him by his own hands.

Adam and Clim overhead this exchange. They readied their bows at the same time, and Adam then shot the Sheriff, while Clim shot the Justice, and both the officials fell down dead before the crowd's eyes. The people fled, and William and Clim quickly untied their sworn-brother. William took up his axe, and the other two took up swords. Fighting as true brothers, they threw many men to the ground. They fought their way to the city gates, and after unlocking them, Adam Bell told the crowd to get a new a porter, and tossed them back their keys, wishing them evil luck.

The three sworn-brothers returned to Inglewood and their trusty greenwood tree. As they were celebrating, they heard a sound of weeping. They found Alice and the three children hiding in the bushes, who stopped crying when they saw that William still lived. The whole reunited company kept their joyous conversation short, as their dinner was still on the hoof.

Later William spoke of a plan he had, to go to the king and ask for his pardon, in return for which the three sworn-brothers would make a promise of peace. The three set off for London, along with the eldest of William's sons, while Alice and the other two children were given to the care of a nunnery.

They reached the court of the king and made their proposal. When the king realized who they were, he had them seized by his officers. But the queen intervened, reminding the king of how he had promised at their marriage that she might have whatever boon she wished. She now wished that the three outlaws be pardoned, and she believed that the three yeomen "true men shall be." The king agreed to her wish.

Immediately after this, two messengers came from the North, bearing with them letters describing the great number of slayings that have taken place in Carlisle, including the deaths of the Justice and the Sheriff. The letters related how the three yeomen must be the most feared archers in all of the North of England. The king was now saddened that he had already pardoned the three sworn-brothers. He was also curious about the abilities of these three men, and arranged an archery contest between them and the royal archers.

The royal shootists set up various targets, and showed good skill, but no better than the three sworn-brothers who matched them at every task. William then boasted that he could shoot a far narrower target. He set up a hazel twig at a distance of twenty score paces, and neatly cleft it in two with his arrow. The king agreed this was the best shooting he had ever seen.

William then announced he would perform a more harrowing stunt—he would shoot an apple off of his own seven-year-old son's head. The king replied that he would allow him to attempt this, but warned that if William failed he would be executed. Furthermore, if the arrow touched the child, or even his gown, all three of the sworn-brothers would be hanged.

William set up a stake and bound his son to it, placing an apple upon his head. He asked his son to turn his head to one side, so that he would not flinch or start when the arrow approached. William then took up his position at a distance of six score paces, and bid the crowd to be quite silent. He shot his arrow, and all assembled saw the apple neatly fall in two. The king then declared that he would never wish to be the target at which William of Cloudsley shot.

The king then made a complete reconciliation with the three sworn-brothers, taking them into his employ. William of Cloudsley was made into the chief royal rider and bowman. The queen made Adam Bell and Clim of the Clough into her yeomen, and even made Alice the chief gentlewoman of her court. And so the sworn-brethren dwelled with the king thereafter, and died good men all three.

THE WISE AND FOOLISH KNIGHTS

The *Gesta Romanorum*, or "Deeds of the Romans" is a collection of stories which dates back as far as the 13th century. It was well-known in its time, and is likely to have influenced later writers of such tales, including Geoffrey Chaucer. Each story is followed by a stated Christian moral, and although the authorship of the collection is uncertain, it is thought to have been used by clerics in some capacity. The following tale centers on a blood-brotherhood. It was accompanied by a specific religious moral, but it also stands on its own.

OF EXCUSES WHICH ARE NOT TO BE ADMITTED IN EXTREME CASES.

From The *Gesta Romanorum*, As Translated By Charles Swan (1824)

The emperor Maximilian was renowned for the wisdom of his government. In his reign, there lived two knights, the one wise and the other foolish, but who had a mutual regard for each other. "Let us make an agreement," said the wise knight, "which will be advantageous to both. The other assented, and by the direction of his friend, proceeded to draw blood from his right arm. "I," said the latter," will drink of thy blood, and thou of mine; so that neither in prosper-

ity or in adversity, shall our covenant be broken, and
whatsoever the one gains, shall be divided with the
other." The foolish knight agreed; and they ratified
the treaty by a draught of each other's blood. After
this, they both dwelt in the same mansion. Now the
lord of that country had two cities, one of which was
built on the summit of a lofty mountain. It was so ordered, that no man could dwell there, unless he possessed great wealth; and having once entered, he must
remain for life. The path to this city was narrow and
stony, and about mid-way, three knights with a large
army were stationed. The custom was that whosoever
passed should do battle, or lose his life, with every
thing that he possessed. In that city, the emperor appointed a seneschal, who received without exception
all who entered, and ministered to them according to
their condition. But the other city was built in a valley
under the mountain, the way to which was perfectly
level and pleasant. Three soldiers dwelt there; who
cheerfully received whomsoever came, and served
them according to their pleasure. In this city also a
seneschal was placed, but he ordered all who approached to be thrown into prison, and on the coming
of the judge to be condemned.

The wise knight said to his companion, "My friend,
let us go through the world as other knights are wont
to do and seek our fortune." His friend acquiesced;
they set out upon their travels, and presently came
to a place where two roads met. "See," said the wise
knight," here are two roads. The one leads to the no-
blest city in the world, and if we go thither, we shall
obtain whatsoever our hearts desire. But the other
path conducts to a city which is built in a valley; if we
venture there, we shall be thrown into prison, and afterwards crucified. I advise, therefore, that we avoid
this road, and pursue the other." "My friend," replied
the foolish knight," I heard long ago of these two cities; but the way to that upon the mountain is very

narrow and dangerous, because of the soldiers who attack those that enter; nay, they frequently rob and murder them. But the other way is open and broad; and the soldiers who are stationed there receive passengers with hospitality, and supply them with all things necessary. This is sufficiently manifest; I see it, and had rather believe my own eyes than you." "It is true," returned his companion," one way is difficult to walk along, but the other is infinitely worse at the end: ignominy and crucifixion will certainly be our doom. But fear you to walk the strait road, on account of a battle, or because of robbers? You, who are a soldier, and therefore in duty bound to fight valiantly! However, if you will go with me the way I desire, I promise to precede you in the attack; and be assured with your aid we shall overcome every obstacle." "I protest to you," said the other, "I will not go your way, but will take mine own." "Well," replied the wise knight, "since I have pledged you my word, and drank your blood in token of fidelity, I will proceed with you, though against my better judgment." So they went by the same path.

Their progress was extremely pleasant, till they reached the station of the three soldiers, who honorably and magnificently entertained them. And here the foolish knight said to the wise one, "Friend, did I not tell thee how comfortable this way would be found; in all which the other is deficient?" "If the end be well," replied he," all is well; but I do not hope it." With the three soldiers they tarried some time; insomuch that the seneschal of the city, hearing that two knights, contrary to royal prohibition, were approaching, sent out troops to apprehend them. The foolish knight he commanded to be bound hand and foot, and thrown into a well, but the other he imprisoned. Now, when the judge arrived, the malefactors were all brought before him, and amongst the rest, our two knights—the wiser of whom thus spoke: "My lord, I complain of my comrade, who is the occasion of my death. I declared to him the law of this city, and the danger to which we were exposed, but he would not listen to my words, nor abide by my counsels. 'I will trust my eyes,' said he, 'rather than you.' Now, because I had taken an oath never to forsake him in prosperity or in adversity, I accompanied him hither. But ought I therefore to die? Pronounce a just judgment." Then the foolish knight addressed the judge: "He is himself the cause of my death. For every one knows that he is reckoned wise, and I am naturally a fool. Ought he then so lightly to have surrendered his wisdom to my folly? And had he not done so, I should have returned to go the way which he went, even for the solemn oath which I had sworn. And therefore, since he is wise, and I am foolish, he is the occasion of my death." The judge, hearing this, spoke to both, but to the wise knight first. "Dost thou deserve to be called wise, who listened so heedlessly to his folly and followed him? And, fool that thou art! Why didst thou not credit his word? By your own egregious folly ye are both justly doomed. And both shall be suspended on the cross." Thus it was done.

The original moral of the story identifies the narrow way as the way of penitence that leads to Heaven, and the broad, alluring way as the worldly path that leads to Hell.

However, there seems to be a secular moral as well. Don't allow loyalty to your blood-brother to lead you into foolishness unnecessarily. If you do decide to follow him even when you know better, then be prepared to take responsibility for your own actions. Loyalty isn't an excuse for stupidity, and it won't absolve you of your misdeeds.

CENTRAL AND EASTERN EUROPE

Blood-brotherhood and other related rites were once quite common among the Magyar and Slavic peoples. The region of the Balkans in particular could be considered a center of blood-brotherhood, as the practice was much more common there than in other parts of Europe, and also survived in some areas as late as the 20th century. Christian priests officiated the custom more often in that region than elsewhere. Blood-brotherhood was also practiced by Muslim peoples in the region, and the reach of the customs extended into Turkey, spread between Eastern Europe and Asia.

Among the Magyars of Hungary, blood-compacts were common in ancient times, and existed at least as late as the sixteenth century. The primitive Hungarian saga of the *Hetu Moger*, "The Seven Magyar," depicts a blood-compact formed on the occasion of the selection of the ninth century chief Almos, the first Grand Prince of the Magyars. The men who swore allegiance to him each let blood flow from his right arm into a basin, swearing to be loyal to Almos and his family, to treat each other as equals, and to fairly share all booty. They also uttered a curse as their blood was flowing that if any were to break the pact, his blood would continue to flow out of him until the vein was empty. A further trace of Magyar blood-compacts is found in an old folk-tale involving a compact between an ogre and a prince. The story relates how they filled a glass half way up with blood from their little fingers, and the latter half with wine, and then drank it together.[1]

An example of blood-brotherhood compact in Romania once occurred between Baldwin II of Courtenay, the last French Emperor of Constantinople in the 13th century, and a people called the *Comans* who had settled in Romania's northeastern region of Moldavia. Baldwin wished to have the Comans' assistance against John III Doukas Vatatzes, Greek Emperor at Nicaea. To ensure good faith on both sides the emperor and his chief men spilled their blood into a silver cup, the Coman King and his chief men doing likewise. The mixed blood was diluted with wine and water and the men of both parties drank from it, saying that they were then blood-brothers. Next, the Comans had a dog cross from the French side to theirs and hacked it to death with their swords. The French followed this by doing the same and both parties said that they too should be so cut to pieces if they failed each other.[2]

In southern Bulgaria, blood-brotherhood was traditionally sealed on St. John's Day. Each of the brothers-to-be prepared a sprig from a certain evergreen tree, a symbol of loyalty. To this was affixed a gold or silver coin, attached by a red thread, which was a symbol of the love and loyalty that the sworn brothers were expected to have for one another. After exchanging the sprigs in the presence of the assembled guests, the two men undertook the blood mixing. The men made wounds in themselves and mutually sucked each other's blood to clarify the tightness of the bond that they were making, and from that moment on they considered themselves blood-relations. Next, the two men stood side-by-side upon the hearth (which some scholars have suggested was a symbol of the men's readiness to leap into the fire for the other), after which the entertainment of the guests would begin. The two men would further kiss each other on the hands, exchange the sprigs once again, and drink wine out of the same bottle, and exchange various gifts. The whole ceremony was repeated exactly one year later, as a renewal of the bond; on this occasion the elder of the two "brothers" would be the host, whereas the younger had been the host the year before. The same friends and family would be invited who had been witnesses to the first ceremony.[3]

Another Bulgarian blood-brotherhood tradition was practiced in the region of the Arda river. The men who intended to become brothers would inform the friends and family and set the date for a festivity, to which many people they knew were to be invited, and which was usually held by the younger of the brothers-to-be. The ceremony itself began with the men cutting themselves on the thumb of the right hand before the witness of the assembled guests, and then mutually sucking up the blood. Then they placed belts upon each other. Those present would give good wishes to the two and seat themselves at the table. From that moment forward the sworn-brothers were considered related.[4]

A form of blood-brotherhood practice among the Bosnians was officiated by a priest. In the ritual the priest would first read a prayer to the future sworn-brothers, which laid emphasis on the mutual duties of the bond. The priest summoned the men to kiss and to repeat an oath after him. The church-servant next brought a goblet of good wine in, and the younger of the two men scratched himself on the right hand until some drops of blood welled up. This blood was mixed with the wine, which the two men drank, thus sealing and confirming their *pobratimstvo*, or sworn-brotherhood.[5] Blood-brotherhood was also practiced among Bosnian Muslims. The two men would scratch themselves on the right arm so that a couple of blood drops appeared and then each licked up the blood of the other with his tongue. From then on they were considered brothers and each would have the greatest willingness to sacrifice his life for that of the other.[6]

Ceremonies of brother-making pobratimstvo were also part of the cultures of Serbia and Macedonia. A common ritual involved the two mean eating salt and bread together, and in addition drinking *rakia* brandy, of which the men had mixed drops of blood from their right arms. The *pobratim* relation in this way created a very tight bond, as the blood-brother was considered as dear in worth as an actual physical brother. Each pobratim had an obligation to protect the other as his dearest possession, and to avenge insults and offences to him.[7] Other forms of the rite in Serbia involved mutual drinking of blood from cuts upon the wrist, exchanges of gifts, and having blessings made on the brotherhood by a priest.[8] The cultural practice of probratimstvo continued rather late in Serbia, at least into the 1970s. It was also believed that an ill man could *draw upon the strength* of his healthy blood-brother. [9]

Blood-brotherhood practices were also a part of the traditional culture of Albania, where they were often employed by two men who needed each other's aid, especially in matters of feuding. To seal their alliance, the two men would prick their fingers with knives, and then mutually lick up each other's blood, or else mix the blood into a glass of rakia which both then drank. The men were then regarded as true blood-relations, their children forbidden to marry each other.[10]

Often in both Albania and Bulgaria the groom of a wedding and his best man, or *vlam,* were expected to be sworn brothers. In the Albanian version, this blood-brotherhood was officiated in a church by a priest, who would say a traditional prayer over the two men. They then would cut themselves and each would swallow a couple of drops of blood from the other. Often the man to become the best man was chosen before any such blood-bond had been created.[11]

An interesting example of a blood-oath made in connection to a mission of vengeance occurred around 1840 in the region of southwestern Montenegro and Dalmatia. A man had killed a young woman who rejected his advances, attacking her while she was alone, tending to her flock. By custom this outrage gave the young woman's family and friends in her village a right of blood-feud. Six men, including the dead woman's brother, her fiance, and the oldest men of her village, all came together to form a vengeance-party, and arrived at the church highly armed to make their oath at the same occasion as the liturgy for the deceased woman.

After the beginning of the communion, the priest bade the six men to come up to the altar. The priest stood before them in his vestments, holding the bread and chalice while the men bowed in a row before them, cut themselves on the index finger of the left hand, and let the blood drip into the chalice. After all of this took place in complete silence, the priest mixed the bread and wine with the blood, and bade the avengers to lift one hand to heaven and to touch the other hand to the clothes of the murder victim, and to repeat an oath. By the long, solemn oath the men obliged themselves to make a vengeance against the family of the murderer, and to make it as bloody as possible. Next, the priest called them to kneel and gave each of them some of the bloodied bread and wine to take as communion. Then the priest lifted the chalice and spoke a prayer, asking God to help the men achieve their earthly justice, and that God punish the faithless inhabitants of the murderer's village with his wrath. In conclusion, the priest imparted his blessing to the avengers.[12]

Some evidence of blood-brotherhood rites in the Ukraine was gathered by Rabbi Petachia of Ratisbon, a Bohemian who made exploratory travels through Eastern Europe, the Caucasus region, Persia and the Middle East in the late twelfth century. He writes that in the region he calls "Kedar," the men often pledged their faith to one another with a blood-rite, especially when two men were travelling together on a journey. One man would stick a needle into his finger, and invited his companion to swallow the blood. The men were then thought to be of the same blood and flesh.[13]

Sworn-brotherhood formed by mixing of blood was also known among the Turks who lived in eastern Bulgaria. After agreeing to become sworn-brothers, the men would cut themselves on a finger and then mutually suck each other's blood. From then on they were called "blood brothers," considered as relatives, yet this bond was even more highly esteemed than natural brotherhood. It was thought that the bond extended not only though life but *into the afterlife,* as well. Despite being considered relatives, men in such a bond were not barred from marriage to each other's female relatives, but it was necessary that one man would have the approval of his "brother" first.[14] A different use for blood rites among the Turks was from an era in which the Turks did not allow

Bulgarians to live among them in Constantinople unless they created a brotherhood with them by blood-mixing.[15]

PRINCE MARKO

The most famous hero in legends of the southern Slavic peoples is Prince Marko, who is celebrated in many Serbian, Romanian, Bulgarian and Macedonian epic poems. The legends about Marko vary from nation to nation, and find their fullest expression in the Serbian *Marko Kralyevich Cycle*, which tells a complete story of his birth, adventures and death. These poems were kept alive for centuries by *gousslari*, traveling bards who recited the stories by memory, accompanying their performance with music from stringed instruments.

In the flesh, Marko Kralyevich was a vassal of the Ottomans, who he loyally served from his castle at Prilip in the 14th century, but the legends of the Marko Cycle make him into a heroic defender of the Serbians. Marko is depicted as having superhuman strength; his primary weapon being a six-edged mace weighing 100 pounds, made of steel, silver and gold, and some claimed his father to be a dragon. He chose his beloved horse Sharatz—with whom he had always shared half of his wine—because it was the only horse he could not throw. The legends allude that Marko is not truly dead, but only sleeping in a cave, awaiting the day he must return.

Two other men in the poems of the Marko Cycle are Milosh of Potzerye and the "winged" Relya of Pazar. Together with Marko, these men make up a trio of heroic knights. They are also all three *pobratimi*, or sworn-brothers. In Serbia, the *pobratim* relationship was often formed by rite involving the drinking of blood mixed with wine.[1]

One legend tells of a conflict between the three versus a fierce figure known as Bogdan the Terrible. The three knights are travelling by horseback to the sea. As they pass through a vineyard, Relya allows his horse to prance wildly, carelessly crushing many of the grapes.

Marko quickly warns him to stop. He relates that he once passed through the same vineyard and crushed the grapes the same way, and Bogdan the Terrible had immediately appeared to punish him. As Marko was the trespasser, he did not think that God would help him to win a fight, so he fled. Sharatz was swifter that Bogdan's steed, but Bogdan was still able to throw his own mace over the growing distance between them, grazing Marko's shoulder.

No sooner does Marko finish this warning than Bogdan appears in the distance, approaching with twelve minions. Marko again wants to flee, but Relya convinces him that it would be shameful for the three heroes not to stand and fight together. It is decided that Relya and Milosh will take on Bogdan himself, while Marko single-handedly takes on the twelve.

Marko soon sends all the twelve crashing to the ground with his massive mace, and quickly has them all with their hands bound behind their backs, driven through the vineyard as prisoners. But then Marko sees that Bogdan has captured the other two heroes in the same manner.

Seeing Bogdan's power, Marko becomes afraid and begins to run. But the next moment he remembers his oath with his two *pobratimi*. All three had pledged to always help one another.

He lowers his helmet and rushes toward Bogdan with his sword drawn. So terrible is his fury that Bogdan's legs tremble beneath him. Bogdan calls for Marko to halt, and offers an exchange of prisoners. Marko consents, and in reconciliation, all of the men share grapes and wine before both parties go their separate ways.

Another of the Serbian legends tells of yet another rescue by Marko. Milosh, and his two friends Milan of Topitzla and Ivan of Kosanchich, travel north of the Danube on a mission to rescue Milan's father from a Magyar ruler General Vucha, who has imprisoned the elder Topitzla. When the three men arrive at Vucha's castle at Varadin, there is a hard battle, and they soon find themselves captured and thrown into a dungeon. There, the polluted water reaches their knees, and the bones of prior prisoners are piled as high as a hero's shoulders.

After three days, Milosh manages to get a passing messenger to give him a scroll on which to write a message to his sworn-brother Marko. He describes the desperate situation, telling Marko that they will not survive three more days, and implores him to make a rescue or ransom. Then, "Milosh scratche[s] his cheek and seal[s] the missive with his blood" [2] and sends the messenger off.

After receiving the message, Marko takes Sharatz north, both swimming through the Danube, and arriving before the castle at Varadin. There, he lays down on the grass, casually drinking red wine, and giving half to Sharatz. He makes a picture of calmness and arrogance.

The daughter-in-law of General Vucha spots Marko, and his appearance is enough to stricken her with a fever to last three years. She rushes to tell Vucha of this bold hero in his wolfskin coat and cap, and great black moustache as large as a yearling lamb. Vucha replies that his dungeon will soon have an additional prisoner.

Vucha sends his son Velimir with a force of 300 men against Marko, but the hero cuts down one hundred, Sharatz tramples another hundred, and the final third are driven into the Danube. Marko finally captures Velimir, binding him hand and foot. Next Vucha himself leads 3000 men against Marko, attacking him from all four directions, but with sword in one hand and spear in the other, Marko defeats them all. Now he captures Vucha himself, brings the two Magyars back with him to Prilip, and throws them into his own dungeon.

Soon the wife of General Vucha writes to Marko, asking what ransom he would ask for her son and her husband. Marko tells her to release Ivan and the Topitzlas, giving them each a great quantity of gold, and to pay Marko as well for his own troubles. As for Milosh, she is to release him and give him whatever he might ask. As a result, Milosh returns home with twelve Arabian horses and a golden carriage; the aged Topitzla rides within, now wearing General Vucha's best Easter Day finery.

In both of these legends, Marko is inspired to his great heroic deeds because of his *pobratim* relationships of sworn-brotherhood, and his commitment to the bond's ideals of mutual assistance and loyalty.

RUSSIAN BOGATYRS

Russian heroic poetry survived as an oral lore for centuries before it began to be recorded by scholars. Its dominant form is the *byliny* (meaning "that which has been"), lengthy epic verse legends that were sung or chanted from memory. These often concern the *bogatyrs*, heroic warrior knights. The largest group of the *byliny* is the Kievan Cycle which depicts legendary events of Kiev when it was the capital of Russia over a thousand years ago, and ruled, as the stories depict it, by "Prince Vladimir the Fair Sun."

In these legends, the most famous bogatyr of Vladimir's court is Ilya of Murom, renown for his wisdom and strength. In a battle with the Tartars, Ilya seizes a Tartar warrior by his lower legs, and swings him like a club to clear out openings in the enemy formations. Ilya is also the slayer of the "Nightingale Robber," a half-human half-bird creature whose song is like a bird's, but which destroys life around it through its sheer volume. Ilya shoots an arrow though the creature's eye, and brings it back half-dead to Kiev. It is ordered to sing for the court at half its strength, but even this proves so destructive that Ilya quickly beheads it.

Another bogatyr of the tales is Dobrynya Nikitich, slayer of a twelve-headed dragon, the Gorynchishche. With the help of Ilya, he also defeats Baba Yaga, "the Witch of the Mountain." A third Bogatyr is Alyosha Popovich, killer of a semi-human dragon, Tugarin. All three men—Ilya, Dobrynya, and Alyosha—are *pobratimy*, sworn-brothers.[1]

One *bylina*, "The Absence of Dobrynya," is not about such heroic feats, but addresses issues of sworn-brotherhood itself. The story begins at a time when Dobrynya is questioning the very worth of his life, asking if it would have been better if he had been killed after his birth. Seeking a change, he decides to leave Kiev on a solitary journey. He informs his wife Natasya that he may be gone for years. If he has not returned in six years, she should consider him as good as dead, and then she may remarry, or else live as a widow if she so pleases. But Dobrynya makes one stipulation: she may not marry his sworn-brother Alyosha. Dobrynya then "rides forth upon the open plain."

Three years pass with no sign or news of Dobrynya, and three years more. Alyosha then appears at the court, bringing word that Dobrynya has died. The prince Vladimir soon encourages Natasya to marry again; she should marry a prince, a boyar, or a hero—or perhaps even "bold Alyosha." She replies that she has satisfied her husband's wish by waiting six years, and she will now fulfill her own wish by waiting six more.

Six more years come and go. Dobrynya's absence has gone on for twelve years altogether. Only then does Natasya heed Prince Vladimir's advice and agree to wed Alyosha. A three-day feast is planned with the marriage ceremony following.

In the story it is then revealed that Dobrynya has been alive the whole time; Alyosha's report to the court was deliberate deception. One day, as he is riding, Alyosha's horse begins to stumble, and will not carry him further. The beast then starts speaking in a human voice, informing him that Natasya and Alyosha are being wed that very day.

Dobrynya rides back to Kiev as swiftly as he can. When he arrives, he learns from his mother about how Alyosha had falsely reported his death. Disguising himself as a musician, he goes to the palace dining hall, where all of the concerned persons are at the feast. He slips his wedding ring into a goblet of green wine that is served to Natasya. Finishing her drink, she is astounded to find the ring. The "musician" then reveals his true identity.

Natasya and Alyosha fall to their knees, begging Dobrynya's forgiveness. He replies that he will forgive Natasya for marrying his sworn-brother, and he will even forgive Alyosha for marrying her. But what he will not forgive is Alyosha's false claim of his death, which brought so many tears to Dobrynya's mother. Dobrynya swiftly metes out punishment:

> "He seized Alyoshka by his yellow curls,
> He dragged Alyoshka over the table of oak,
> He flung Alyoshka about the brick-built floor,
> He seized his riding-whip,
> And set about belaboring him with the butt-end.
> You could not distinguish between
> the blows and the groans."
>
> *(verses 320–325)*[2]

The last part of the bylina tells of Dobryna and Natasya's continuing happiness together, and expresses the wish that as unscrupulous a man as Alyosha should never have the fortune of marrying at all.

BLOOD RITUALS OF THE ARABS

Blood-brotherhood and other blood-rituals have been practiced by Arabic peoples from the Arabian Peninsula, the Levant, and even North Africa. These practices have their roots as far back as pre-Islamic times, but some lasted nearly to modern times. There have also been highly similar rituals with use of blood that seem to follow the general patterns of blood-oaths. Some of the rituals have also involved religious locations and objects.

Some very early evidence comes from fifth century BCE Greek writer Herodotus, who described an Arab blood-oath of friendship in his *Histories*. The two men making the pledge were both cut on their hands by the thumbs, and the blood was then smeared on seven sacred stones set on the ground between them. Invocations were meanwhile made to the god Orotalt and the goddess Alilat.[1]

A blood-brotherhood rite that survived into the 19th century among the Syrians was known as the "Covenant of Blood" (*m'ahadat ed-dam*) and the men who made use of it "Brothers of the Covenant" (*akhwat el-m'ahadah*). The two men would call together relatives and neighbors who were to bear witness to the sealing of their compact. Their oaths were written down in duplicate and signed by both men, and also by the witnesses. One man then opened a vein in the other's arm, and inserted a quill in the vein, through which he sucked the blood out. The blood remaining on the blade used to make the cut was then wiped onto one of the covenant-papers The second man then repeated this with the first man's arm. The two then declared, "We are brothers in a covenant made before God; who deceiveth the other, him will God deceive." Each of the papers was then folded and sewn up into a small leather case about an inch square, known as "the House of the Amulet" (*bayt hejab*), which the men would wear hanging from the neck or upon the arm.

This bond was considered greater than marriage, as marriage could end in divorce, but the blood-bond could not be dissolved. It was also stronger than natural brotherhood. Siblings were called "milk-brothers" or "suckling brothers," as connected by common milk; the created connection of blood was thought stronger still. The blood-brothers thought themselves possessors of a double life, as each man was ready to lay down his life for the other, or with him. In fact, the blood was taken from the upper arm in the ceremony because the arm represented a man's strength. The blood covenant was often used by business partners acting in confidence, by conspirators and robbers, yet also was the chosen compact of loving friends.[2]

At Mecca, oaths of mutual protection were created or dissolved at the Kaaba, the cubical granite building which is Islam's most sacred site, and which was previously a pagan shrine. One form of such a life and death covenant involved each party dipping their hands into a pan filled with blood and then tasting it. Clans who had formed alliances this way were known as "blood-lickers" (*la'akat al-dam*). Two similar forms of covenant-making existing at about the same time at Mecca involved fluids other than blood. One involved washing the corners of the Kaaba with water from the Zamzam Well and then drinking it, while another involved the parties dipping their hands into perfume and the wiping the Kaaba with it.[3]

A custom that survived rather late in some parts of Arabia was practiced when one man sought the protection of another. He would release his own blood, and wipe it on the doorpost of the man whose favor he entreated. This act was also a gesture of self-deprecation and atonement.[4]

An example of a blood-brotherhood ritual among the Arabs in North Africa occurred in Tripoli in 1790 between the local Bey and a dignitary. The two men already had sworn allegiance, but wished to confirm their oaths more strongly. They went to a local mosque, and at the altar they swore over the Qur'an that each would hold the other's life as sacred. Then they wounded themselves, and mixed their blood in a vessel, and both sipped from it.[5]

Another blood ritual practiced among the Arabs was one where blood was not drunk, but merely smeared on the face and body. One example from the early sixth century involved Abdullah ibn K'ab, leader of the Christian Beni Harith community at Najran in southwestern Arabia, who was slain by the Jewish warrior Dhu Nowas in an act of religious persecution. As he received the death stroke at his execution, his fellow sufferers, who also were to be executed, ran up to him to catch up the blood and smear it upon themselves. The purpose of such an act was to tightly unify oneself with the person whose blood was spilled, and so to go with them in death.[6]

Blood-oaths were purported to have been practiced by the Qahtan tribe of the southern region of the Arabian Peninsula. The Qahtan were highly feared by others in the Nejd central highland region, and were the topic of many rumors. It was said by the Nejd highlanders that the Qahtan cannibalized their enemies, and happily declared the rump to be the best roast; that they did not let one of their men marry until he had killed an enemy; that they were vicious enough to kill a man merely for inhaling smoke from their fires. It was also said that the Qahtan would solemnize their oaths by drinking human gore.[7] Since these rumors about the Qahtan were not actually substantiated by researchers, however, this last idea can only be seen as an example of Arabian lore about blood-rites.

THE EPIC OF GILGAMESH

Discovered upon stone tablets among the ruins of the ancient Assyrian city of Nineveh in the mid-nineteenth century, *The Epic of Gilgamesh* is thought to be the oldest epic verse in human literature, possibly written earlier than 2000 BCE. With various versions in different ancient languages, ages and locations, the tale of a semi-divine king seems to have once been popular throughout the ancient Middle East. Containing a sub-plot description of a world-wide flood remarkably like the one depicted in the Bible, *Gilgamesh* shocked Victorian Era scholars, who had not yet imagined any Hebrew scripture could possibly have pagan origins. An actual historic king Gilgamesh of Uruk existed, but certainly did not have the adventures the poem ascribes to him. It is unknown whether any foster-brother was as central to his life as one was to his mythic counterpart.

Gilgamesh, son of the goddess Ninsun, is king of the city of Uruk. He proudly boasts to being two-thirds divine and one-third human, and is the both the world's greatest king and the world's strongest super-human. He is a young king, and is cruel and repressive to the people of Uruk. He forces them to labor intensely building the walls of the city. Another of his cruelties is his demand to take the virginity of all newlywed brides of Uruk. The people of Uruk pray to the gods for deliverance from their ruler.

The Gods make a mysterious response. One day, a trapper discovers a strange hairy wild-man living with the animals outside the city. This creature is Enkidu, an opposite of Gilgamesh, being one-third human and two-thirds beast, but also supremely strong. A temple prostitute, Shamhat, sexually seduces Enkidu, giving her a way to keep the semi-human near so that he can be introduced to the ways of the city and civilization. He learns his lessons, taking up language, clothing, and other human advantages. He also soon realizes the injustice of Uruk's king.

Gilgamesh has two strange dreams. In the first, a great meteor falls to earth, so large that he cannot move it. But then, he embraces it affectionately. The second dream is similar; an oversized axe is outside Gilgamesh's door, which he cannot even lift, but finally he embraces it.

One day, Gilgamesh is about to enter a marriage-hall to have his way with a virgin bride, when Enkidu appears and confronts him. They fight and wrestle for a long time, until Enkidu submits to Gilgamesh—or, in some interpretations of the myth, until they find themselves perfectly matched, none able to overcome the other. Then they kiss and become friends.

The two make a plan for an adventure: they will go to the great Cedar Forest in Persia and kill its guardian, the demon Humbaba, who has stopped the lumber of that wood from being used for the building of Uruk's walls. Before they set out on their journey, Ninsun adopts Enkidu as her son. Thus Gilgamesh and Endkidu have become not only friends, but also adult foster-brothers.

Their journey lasts six days and five nights, and Gilgamesh has an ominous dream on each of the nights, but Enkidu cleverly interprets each one to predict success. When they enter the forest, Enkidu loses his courage and starts to run, and Gilgamesh must wrestle him to the ground and convince him to stand together against the demon. He says to Enkidu, "A slippery path is not feared by two people who help each other. [...] A three-ply rope cannot be cut. The mighty lion—two cubs can roll him over." [1]

After the forest's guardian approaches them and argues with
them, showing them a face of horror, Gilgamesh becomes afraid
and hides, and it is now Enkidu who must shout encouragement
to his foster-brother. Soon, with the aid of winds sent by the sun-
god Shamash, Gilgamesh subdues Humbaba, who begs for his
life, offering to become Gilgamesh's servant, but Enkidu tells
Gilgamesh that his fame will be the greater if he just kills the
demon. Gilgamesh decapitates him, and the severed head shouts
curses upon Enkidu before it dies.

Now Gilgamesh is so world-famed that even the love-goddess
Ishtar wishes to become his consort. Gilgamesh spurns her,
recounting the long list of men she's had and ruined. Insulted,
Ishtar sends the Bull of Heaven upon Uruk. Its rumbling and
breath open up cracks in the earth that swallow hundreds of
Uruk's people, but the two foster-brothers defeat it and cut off its
head. Enkidu even warns Ishtar that she could be next, flinging
one of the bull's legs in her face.

Gilgamesh and Enkidu's time of heroic adventure together is
short. The gods decide that someone must pay for the deaths of
Humbaba and the Bull of Heaven, and single out Enkidu, who
suffers for twelve days before he dies. Gilgamesh raises up a
poetic lament, ordering all people and beasts, and even all the
trees and lands and rivers, to cry out in mourning. Gilgamesh
orders a monumental statue of the most precious materials to
be built in Enkidu's likeness. Soon Gilgamesh contemplates his
own mortality. He decides to seek the counsel of Utnapishtim, the
"Far-Away," the man who was king of the world before the great
world-destroying flood. He and his wife were the only survivors,
and the only human beings to have been granted immortality by
the gods.

To find him, Gilgamesh must wander to the ends of the earth.
He travels beyond Mount Mashu, where two giant scorpions guard
the rising and setting of the sun. He sails over the Waters of Death,
one touch of which would kill him. When he finds Utnapishtim,
he is told by the old man that the gods will never again grant

immortality to any mortal, but Gilgamesh might gain it by either of two difficult tasks. The first is to stay fully awake for six days and seven nights—which Gilgamesh utterly fails at. The second is to retrieve and eat a unique life-giving plant from the bottom of the ocean. Gilgamesh is able to get the plant, but a snake steals it from him before he can use it. The snake eats the plant itself, and sheds its old skin as it slithers away. The king of Uruk now accepts his mortality, and becomes content with the worldly success of building the great walls of the city. The arrogant and cruel demi-god is humbled, and thus the prayers of the people of Uruk are answered.

With one man being semi-divine, and the other semi-bestial, the story is one of united opposites, but also is about men who regard each other as peers. Both Gilgamesh and Enkidu become more human as result of their experiences. The story is also an example of the common theme of brotherhood forming between men who once were evenly matched enemies, who gain each other's mutual respect. The dynamics of the combined strength of the male-bond is dramatized in the episode of the battle with Humbaba, each foster-brother giving the other courage at the moments when the other's courage flags. Brotherhood is stronger than the sum of its parts.

BLOOD-OATHS &
SWORN BROTHERHOOD IN ASIA

Blood oaths, sworn-brotherhood, and blood-brotherhood have had a widespread presence throughout most of the vast region of Asia. The practices have been part of the cultures of central Asia and cultures of the mountainous territories. They have also been part of the traditions of eastern Asia and Indochina. The lengthy history of China also has examples of these customs through many of its historical periods.

Among the Lepcha people of the north Indian state of Sikkim, a relationship of *ingzong,* meaning "like a younger brother," was created by a blood-rite. A pig was killed and the intestines offered to the god Komsithing, who was supposed to have invented the ingzong relationship. The men then ate the pork and swore to always love and help each other. A second stage of the ritual was officiated by an elderly man, who prepared a cup of hot millet beer (*chi*) with daubs of butter on its rim. The old man told the ingzong of the importance of the occasion, and warned how Komsithing would send the demon Sankyoor Moong to punish any man who betrayed the oath. The men then drank the chi and ate the butter. This bond was often used to secure trade agreements with neighboring peoples, but even then it had much of the same effects as biological brotherhood; marriage between the men's descendants was forbidden for nine generations.[1]

There is evidence that blood-oaths were made by men of the Northern Indian state of Ladakh, a region so influenced by Tibetan culture that it is sometimes called "Little Tibet." A Ladakh legend mentions a man who wrote a contract in his blood, and kept the document hidden under his horse's saddle.[2] In Tibet itself, blood-brotherhood was sealed by blending the blood of the contracting parties, and then the drinking of it.[3]

In Nepal, a *mit* relationship was a ritually created sworn brotherhood; the men who did it were considered as sons of the same father, and their children were prohibited from marrying each other. While the practical benefit of mutual aid between the brothers was one reason for making the bond, mutual affection was the primary reason.

The best day for the ritual was selected by astrological auspices. The ceremony was usually officiated by a Brahmin priest. The two men removed their footwear and their great curved kukri knives. They faced each other across a sacred fire, on which rice, honey, and butter were burned. The men made exchanges of coins and some articles of clothing. Bits of grass, flowers, or rice and curds were placed upon the men. The priest then told them to be true to one another, making reference to Sugriva, the mythological Hindu Monkey-King who became loyal to Rama when the latter went on a quest to defeat the demon-king Ravanna. The priest announced that the two men were thenceforth brothers. The ritual sometimes ended with the two bathing together in a sacred river or pool, and was followed by a feast.[4]

Blood-oaths were practiced among the Xiongnu, a nomadic people of Central Asia, whose height of power occurred over a thousand years before that of the Mongols. Once in 49 BCE, a Xiongnu leader or *zenghi* named Hun-han-ya wished to strengthen his position against his rivals by forming an alliance with some ambassadors of the Chinese emperor, Yüan-ti. The zenghi and the envoys went up to the top of a hill and killed a white horse, and then the zenghi took a knife, some gold, and a rice spoon, and used them to mix the blood with wine. The Xiongnu and the ambassadors drank the mixture from a human skull, taken from a king of the neighboring Yuezhi people who had been slain by a previous zenghi.[5]

Blood-brotherhood practices existed among the Mongols. The men who would become sworn-brothers, or *anda*, mingled their blood in a goblet where it was also "mixed with gold," that is, some piece of gold, such as a coin was also placed in the cup. The blood might also be mixed with brandy. After this, the men exchanged their clothing.[6] The bond of andas was considered even stronger than that between natural brothers, because of its freely chosen nature.[7] Such an anda bond existed between Genghis Khan and Jamukha who first became friends in their childhood, and which may be history's most significant blood-brotherhood.

Among the Monguor people, who live in north-west China, blood-brotherhood was used either as a promise of general aid, or else for more specific purposes. Two or more men might make the oath together. In the ritual, a sheep, goat, or chicken was killed, and its blood was mixed with wine in a bowl. The men then bowed down before a picture of the temple deity, or "Heaven and all the spirits," while holding burning incense in their joined hands. They then bowed down to each other while swearing mutual aid, and calling on the sprits to punish the disloyal. The men then placed a picture of the invoked god, or a prayer book on the other's head, and then drank the sacrificial blood. After this the new brothers made gifts of clothing to each other.[8] An interesting variation on this oath was a case where three young men, who were already sworn-brothers together, sacrificed a goat in making a fourth older man their "sworn father."[9]

Oath-making rituals, including blood-oaths, were common in traditional Chinese society. Such oaths could be used for any number of purposes, a created blood-brotherhood being just one possibility. The blood oath practices go back at least as far as the Spring and Autumn Period (771–481 BCE). In the Chinese form, sacrifices were made upon an earthen altar, while calling upon spirits and ancestors to witness the occasion of the oath and to punish oath-breakers. A great variety of sacrificial animals were used, such as horses, goats, cows and chickens. Human sacrifices also occurred. Blood from the sacrifices was placed both on the lips of those making the oath, and upon a written document defining the terms of the agreement, which was buried along with the victim after being read out loud to the gods. The participants finally sealed the oath by collectively drinking the victim's blood.[10] In the subsequent Warring States period (481-221 BCE) there was increasing emphasis on the written portion of these rituals, and this trend continued through the Han Dynasty (206 BCE - 220 CE). After this, there is little evidence of blood-oaths until much later, in the late Yuan period (1271–1368).[11]

From the Yuan to the 20th century, Chinese methods of performing a blood-oath were very diverse. Many different sorts of animals were used in sacrifice. A white cockerel was often used, symbolizing the rising morning sun, and thus the return of life. Another common animal selection was to sacrifice a white horse to Heaven, and a black ox to Earth. Eels' blood was even used, to symbolize the blood of dragons. Finally, the human blood of the oath-makers themselves was deployed. Blood represented the *force of life*, and thus could "give life" to ritual objects, by application, or to the very words spoken in an oath, by its consumption.[12]

In 18th century China blood was often consumed with liquor, which "Unites the Hearts." Here it is the shared liquor which signifies the bond; the blood has the power to add strength to the ritual.[13]

Chinese blood-oaths were often performed before deities, such as Heaven and Earth, which was done by performing the ritual on an earthen altar beneath the open sky. Blood-oaths were sometimes also performed before the temple of a local city-god. The red-skinned general Guan Di of the *Romance of the Three Kingdoms* was also often invoked. The deities were expected to bring on the punishment of oath-breakers. The oaths often included fearsome maledictions involving disease, natural disasters, death, descent into hell, or even reincarnation as animals. Whenever sacrificial animals were used in the ritual, there might be a curse made, warning that any betrayer of the oath would share the dying animal's fate.[14]

Although swearing of brotherhood was a common use of this type of blood-bond in China, the blood rite could have any sort of use. In World War Two, the Chinese Communist Party used blood-oaths when getting Chinese citizens to promise not to collude with the invading Japanese.[15]

Among several Chinese cultures that were not of the dominant Han ethnicity, the forms of blood-oath rituals were similar, but often involved the parties passing through a constructed gate of swords, which may have had a maledictive meaning.[16]

Chinese Triad groups, criminal secret societies that also functioned as mutual aid networks, used blood rituals in their initiation ceremonies which followed the general pattern of Chinese blood oaths. This caused some confusion among officials who sometimes assumed that anyone using such a blood-oath must have been involved with the Triads. The Triad rituals involved drinking blood mixed with liquor, the blood coming from sacrificial animals, especially a white cockerel, from the human participants, or sometimes both. Oaths of loyalty were reinforced with dramatic maledictions. Eventually the oaths were elaborated into a lengthy set list of "the Thirty-Six Oaths," each with a specific curse for the disloyal mentioned. The oaths in the Triad rituals might be written down, and then burned in the ceremony. A passage through a gate of swords was ordinarily part of the ritual. The Gods of Heaven and Earth were called upon, and sometimes also Guan Di. Particular to the Triad rituals was an act to call upon the legendary "Five Ancestors" who were said to have formed the first of the Triad groups.[17]

Customs of swearing brotherhood are part of the cultural practices of Taiwan. A group of friends who swear brotherhood hold a feast at the house of one of the "brothers," afterwards switching the feast to a different member's house on following anniversary days. They may also swear loyalty to the war deity

Guan Di, or some other supernatural patron. An image of the
god is purchased at the first ceremony, and moved to the other
brothers' altars subsequently. The sworn brothers use appropriate
kinship terms for each other and also for members of each other's
families.[18]

Among the Miao people (also known as Hmong) of south-
east China and Indochina, a blood-brotherhood rite consisted
of sacrificing a cat or a dog and mixing its blood with wine and
drinking it. [19]

Among the Karen people of Burma and Thailand, there were
three differing levels of brotherhood or truce that could be formed
by three different customs. The first ritual was simply the sharing
of a meal; this signified a truce between men of different tribes, but
could be quite temporary. The second ritual was the planting of a
tree, which meant that the contractors were forming an alliance
that was to last as long as the tree lived. The third ritual was the
blood-covenant itself. The men would cut themselves on the thigh,
mix the blood, and then bring the blood to their lips with their
fingertips. This was a bond of the greatest force, be it made for
peace, or a promise of mutual aid; no appeal for help made on the
basis of this covenant was ever to be disregarded.[20]

Another version of the blood-bond among some Karen tribes
was called "drinking truth." Two chiefs both cut their arms and
mixed their blood in a vessel with whiskey and then drank from
it, thus promising that they and their descendants would be true
to one another for seven generations.[21]

There is also some evidence of blood-bonds among the Shan
ethnicity, located mostly in Burma. Once some Shan men who
were forming a plot to commit a murder and robbery pledged
their loyalty to their cause by drinking the blood of the plot's
leader, mixed with whiskey or a rice beer.[22]

Covenants of friendship in Thailand were sometimes formed by a blood-ritual where the men drank blood directly from wounds that they had made on their bodies.[23]

In addition to the Hmong people mentioned above, several other ethnicities of Vietnam had blood-bond and sworn-brother customs, some surviving to contemporary times. Among the Roglai, a blood-ritual is used to promise enduring friendship and mutual aid, the blood of the parties being mixed with alcohol and then drunk. A different ritual with the same meaning is simply to smoke together. To specifically create sworn-brotherhood in a ritual is known as *twaq yut*, and just like actual brothers, each man will care for the other's children if their father should die. It is possible for a Roglai to join in a neighboring ethnic group by a blood-ritual. One such alliance involved sharing a meal of pork and rice, and mutual drinking of blood. As the Roglai explain it, "when two people mix blood they become one body."[24]

Among Vietnam's Katu people, villages involved in feuding can sometimes repair their relations by having a ritual *teeng tabah*, a large feast at which the headmen of the villages ritually drink the blood of a buffalo together.[25] Among the Bru, blood rituals can sometimes be used by men of one *sau* (a patrilineal grouping larger than a family) to join another. Both the men joining and those receiving them cut their fingers, letting the blood drip into rice alcohol which all then drink.[26]

A form of blood-brotherhood ritual once used in Korea was fashioned after the sorts used in China. An historic example occurred after the first Manchu invasion of Korea in 1627. At the end of the war the Manchu prince and King Injo of Korea swore eternal friendship by sacrificing and immolating a black bull and a white horse, burning incense before Heaven and Earth, and contracting blood-brotherhood to keep the peace between them and to aid each other against all mutual dangers.[27]

In early 20th century Korea, a vogue for blood-brotherhood occurred among Korean youths. The fashionable form of the ritual involved the two young men making matching tattoos on each other's arms with carbon soot, and then stating a pledge to each other with their arms crossed. One notable Korean who did this as a boy was Park Chung-hee, who grew up to become dictator of South Korea in the 1960s and 70s.[28]

In Japan, a *keppan* or "blood seal" was once used in making oaths or even on legally binding documents. A wound was made on a fingertip, which was used to make a fingerprint on a document, underneath the oath-maker's signature. Documents with this seal were considered sacredly binding, with divine vengeance to come upon those who broke their promises. It was often used in oaths of fealty and agreements of peace.[29] Such keppan blood-seals were frequently used by men in ceremonies to swear loyalty to martial arts societies. Another form of blood contract used in Japan was the *kessho* or "blood-writing," where the words of the contract were actually written in blood, or else in blood mixed with ink.[30]

GENGHIS KHAN

Genghis Khan, named Temujin at his birth circa 1162, was the founder and ruler of the Mongolian nation, and after his death was named as Grand Khan of the Mongol Empire. The Mongol Empire was second in size only to the British Empire, and was the largest empire extending on a continuous landmass. Many facts about Genghis Khan's early life are obscure, and much of what is known comes from *The Secret History of the Mongols*, a work which was written a few years after his death. The accuracy of the *Secret History* is uncertain; it contains some supernatural material but most of it is at least plausible. It tells the story of the dramatic rise of a young man from destitution to greatness. Critical to the story are two blood-brotherhood relationships. Called *anda,* such bonds were created in Mongolian society by a blood drinking ceremony.[1]

At the time of Temujin's birth, the name of "Mongol" only referred to one of the many tribes of the Mongolian steppe. Temujin was born into the ruling clan of the tribe, the Borjigin, and his father Yesugei was its head. The Borjigin's position as head clan was often contested by the rival clan of the Taichiut. Temujin's mother Hoelun had actually been kidnapped away from her husband of the Merkit tribe, and was thus wed to Yesugei by force. The *Secret History* says that Temujin was born holding a blood-clot in his fist, an omen that the boy was fated to become a great warrior.

At the age of nine, Temujin was taken by his father to visit Deisechen of the Ongirat tribe, with the intention of seeing if Deisechen's young daughter Borte would make a good future bride for Temujin. The two children took a liking to each other, and were promised to each other. Temujin was to stay as a servant of Deisechen for several years as way of paying the bride-price.

However, Temujin soon returned home after Yesugei was poisoned by a band of Tatars. The Taichiut seized power from the weakened Borjigin, and abandoned them. Temujin's small family then lived in extreme poverty, living off of wild roots, rodents and fish. This was a low position for the boy whose legendary original ancestor was the divine "blue-grey wolf."

It was in these difficult years that Temujin became friends with another boy named Jamukha. The two became *andas*, exchanging simple gifts of knucklebones used in games. A year later, they renewed this bond, then exchanging gifts of arrowheads. But in time Jamukha left the region, becoming allied with the powerful Kereit tribe, whose leader Ong Khan (or Toghril) happened to have been *anda* with the late Yesugei.

The nadir of Temujin's life came when the Taichiut raided the Borjigin and enslaved him. He was placed in a *cangue*, a wide wooden collar which made it impossible for the wearer to feed himself. But Temujin was clever and resourceful. He hit an inattentive guard on the head with the cangue itself, and ran. Soon after, some allies of Temujin among the Taichiut hid him in cart of wool, and he was eventually able to escape back to his home.

When he turned sixteen he was able to claim his wife Borte. She brought with her an expensive black sable overcoat, which would have been a gift to her father-in-law. Temujin took the sable to Ong Khan, saying to him, "In old days you and my father became bond-brothers, so you count as my father." [2] Ong Khan accepted the gift, making Temujin a fictive son and henceforth making the Borjigin allies of the Kereit.

One day, the Borjigin were attacked by the Merkit tribe, and Borte was kidnapped as vengeance for the theft of Hoelun from the Merkit many years previously. Temujin's response to this crisis would change the course of his life. He went to Ong Khan, and asked him to join him in a raid on the Merkit. Ong Khan agreed, and also had Jamukha add forces to the effort. The raid was successful, and Borte was rescued.

This adventure brought Temujin and Jamukha back together after they had been separated for many years. They recalled how they had become *andas* in their youth, and saying "when two men become bond-brothers it is as though they had but one life between them,"[3] they decide to renew their vow. As Jamukha would later describe the occasion in the *Secret History*, "We drank the drink that cannot be digested, spoke the words that cannot be forgotten."[4] They exchanged gifts of fine horses, and also traded some of their clothing, the golden sashes they wore at their waists. The ceremony was concluded by sleeping together under one blanket.

Temujin thus exchanged the life of a hunter for that of a steppe warrior. Together he and Jamukha began to gain control of a number of clans. However, a split occurred between the two men after only a year and a half. Jamukha had the same high ambitions as Temujin, and Jamukha was not willing to share his ruling position with him. They went separate ways, and their Mongol followers each had to choose which of the two men to support. Jamukha was able to build powerful alliances with the Merkit, Oirat, and Naiman tribes.

Temujin continued to unite many of the other clans of the Mongol tribe, and after succeeding, took the title of Genghis (or Chingis) Khan. Just one year later, in 1190, the two *andas* came into battle and Jamukha's army forced Genghis and his followers to flee across the steppe.

In 1196, Ong Khan and Genghis made a successful attack on the Tatar tribe in the eastern part of the steppe. In the next year, Genghis defeated the Jurkin tribe. In a radical innovation in steppe warfare, Genghis had the Jurkin leaders executed, and the remaining Jurkin people distributed among the households of his own clans, to unify the two peoples permanently.

Jamukha had been gaining allies as well in the meantime, and in 1201 he audaciously took the title of Gur-Khan, an ancient name meaning "khan of khans." Soon there was another battle between Jamukha's forces and those of Ong Khan and Genghis. Jamukha's army was routed, and in the process Genghis was able to defeat the Taichiut clan which had enslaved him so long before.

In 1202, Ong Khan sent Genghis on a mission to make a second and decisive attack on the Tatars, at which he succeeded, thus avenging his father. Again Genghis deployed the policy of absorbing the surviving Tatars into his own tribe. He established further innovations. No soldiers were to loot any camps until a total victory had been completed. Genghis also organized his soldiers into squads of ten, called *arban*, whose members were meant to be more loyal to one another than to their own kin.

The alliance between Genghis and his fictive father Ong Khan was not to last forever. Ong Khan's actual son Senggum resented the favored position that Genghis had gained, and was able to persuade his father to stop supporting the rising conqueror. Not long after, Genghis' army was fighting the forces of Jamukha and Ong Khan's Kereit warriors combined. The Mongols were able to defeat the Kereit, and Jamukha fled west to remain with the tribe of the Naiman. Ong Khan also attempted this, but was inadvertently killed by a Naiman border guard.

The last large battle for control of the Mongolian territory occurred in 1204. The Mongol forces were smaller in number than the Naiman, but Genghis deployed craftier military tactics. The Mongols used a long line of bowmen, who would fire their arrows and then fall back, replaced by another line. The Naiman answered this by arranging themselves in a similar long, thin defensive line—and then the Mongols sent through a "chisel" formation which divided the Naiman in two. Confused and uncoordinated, many of the Naiman fled in the night, and the remainder were easily defeated in the morning.

Among those who fled was Jamukha. He had only a handful of comrades remaining, and was reduced to living by banditry and hunting in the forest. Soon his own few men betrayed him, seizing him and transporting him to Genghis.

According the the *Secret History*, Genghis was incensed by this act of betrayal, and had Jamukha's false friends executed. Genghis then offered Jamukha a final chance to renew their old *anda* relationship. But Jamukha thought that he could never again be comrades with Genghis, for he would always be an irritant to him, and said that it would be better to be killed. Jamukha vowed that if he were to be killed without any spilling of his blood, he would become protector of Genghis and his descendants forever. Genghis agreed to this condition, and had Jamukha executed bloodlessly.

Having united all of the Mongolian tribes, Genghis was named Grand Khan, or *Khagan*, in 1206. He soon began the imperial conquest of non-Mongolian peoples, waging war against the Tangut Empire and Jin dynasties in China, and against the Kara Khitai Khanate and the Khwarezmid Empire of central Asia. Genghis died in 1227, after the defeat of the Tangut. His sons and grandsons continued to expand the Mongol Empire. At its height in the late thirteenth century, the empire possessed China and Korea in the east, extended through Persia into Iraq in the south, and in the west possessed most of Russia and reached nearly as far as Vienna.

Mongol, the 2007 biopic that tells Genghis Khan's story, prominently features his relationship with Jamukha and serves as one of the most evocative filmed demonstrations of blood-brotherhood in recent cinema. The technique used for the first blood-brotherhood between Temujin and Jamukha differs in the film, but it remains consistent with the blood drinking techniques historically attributed to the Mongols and other rites described elsewhere this survey. The two boys each sliced their own hands and allowed a few drops of blood to fall into a bowl of milk, which they both then drank from. When the two meet again as adults, they exchange gifts, and are actually shown waking up under the same blanket after a long night of singing and drinking. It is important here to avoid the temptation to project twentieth century homoerotic overtones onto the sharing of a blanket, which was more likely another symbolic act of mutual trust and male friendship between the two men. It may even be a symbolic imitation of natural brotherhood, as boys who were brothers would often sleep in the same bed in times long before modern heating. The film also shows some tension between Jamukha and his biological brother over his loyalty to Temujin, and this corresponds to the historically common style of blood-brotherhood that gives preference to blood-brothers over loyalties to one's biological family. As in the traditional telling of Khan's story, Temujin and Jamukha end up fighting against one another, which is also a theme seen before. For these reasons, the film *Mongol* is highly recommended as an illustrative video supplement to this presentation of blood-brotherhood as a rite of male bonding and alliance.[5]

THE ROMANCE
OF THE THREE KINGDOMS

Written in the fourteenth century, the *Romance of the Three Kingdoms* is one of the great classics of Chinese literature. Attributed to Luo Guanzhong, the *Three Kingdoms* is a historic novel, blending fact with legend. It depicts events of an unstable time in Chinese history, the end of the Han Dynasty (206 BCE–220 CE) and the Three Kingdoms period (220–280 CE). The novel is great in length and detail. The opening chapter describes the motivations and manner of the legendary "Peach Garden Oath," a triple blood-brotherhood which is a famous motif of Chinese culture.

The *Romance* begins with a depiction of the instability of the Han rule. A series of Han emperors have allowed the affairs of state to be run by the advice of the cadre of palace eunuchs. There are mysterious signs of the wrongness of this influence of effeminates over the government, such as an earthquake and a tidal wave. There is also a strange sign of many hens developing the characteristics of roosters. A mood of rebellion against the Han develops among much of the population.

Into this situation comes one Chang Chio, a doctor who receives some obscure magical texts from a mysterious old man. Chio studies them, and learns the power to control the winds and the rains. A cult develops around him, and he takes on the title of "Wise and Good Master." His followers incite the Yellow Turban rebellion, which promises to bring not only the fall of the Han, but a new era of heaven and earth; the very blue of heaven would change to yellow. Their army begins to make some headway.

There are, however, many who would prefer stability over chaos. The Prefect of Yuchow, Liu Yan, seeks to enlist men to crush the rebellion. One man who reads Liu Yan's posted notice is Liu Bei, who is a man of learning, with distinguished ancestors, but who has grown up relatively poor. He is very tall, with arms that hang past his knees, and eyes so protuberant that he doesn't need to turn his head to see behind him. As he is reading the notice, he is met by Zhang Fei, a large man with a great booming voice, who is a butcher and wine-seller. The two agree about the need for someone to restore peace, and go to a tavern to talk about how they might raise men. There they meet Guan Yu, a huge man with a great long beard, who has been a fugitive from the law after killing a man. He also joins their project.

The next day the three men go to the garden at the farm of Zhang Fei, where the peach trees are all in bloom. They make a blood-oath of brotherhood, using the sacrificial blood of a black ox and a white horse, and ceremonial wine. Standing amid the incense smoke, they pronounce an oath:

> "We three, though of separate ancestry, join in brotherhood here, combining strength and purpose, to relieve the present crisis. We will perform our duty to the Emperor and protect the common folk of the land. We dare not hope to be together always but hereby vow to die the selfsame day. Let shining Heaven above and the fruitful land below bear witness to our resolve. May Heaven and man scourge whosoever fails this vow."[1]

Liu Bei becomes the eldest brother, Zhang Fei the youngest brother, and Guan Yu the middle-brother. They start to receive help from others, and soon are outfitted with armor and weapons. Liu Bei has a pair of matched swords, Guan Yu has a curved sword, and Zhang Fei a great spear. They continue to find more men, and by the end of the first chapter of the *Three Kingdoms* the fight against the Yellow Turbans has begun.

The three blood-brothers and their oath are frequently the subjects of painting and sculpture. Liu Bei, Guan Yu, and Zhang Fei are often respectively represented with white, red, and black skin, or sometimes with great beards in those colors. These popular artworks are sometimes displayed by businessmen as statements of loyalty and ambition. Over the centuries, the three are also elevated to the status of deities, with Guan Yu being the most powerful of them, and given the name of Guan Di, or Guan Gong. He is pictured as a general with crimson skin and a forked black beard, and often is shown sitting upon a tiger skin. Guan Di is a god of war, but one who prefers the peace that can be kept by readiness for war. He is also a god of wealth and of literature. Guan Di is the tutelary deity of the police, but he is also frequently the favorite god of criminal secret societies like the Triads, who still use oaths fashioned after the Peach Garden Oath in their initiations.[2] It would seem ironic for both police and criminals to be associated with the same god, but the apparent common link is that both groups are men of action and risk, bound by loyalty, like Guan Di and his two blood-brothers themselves.

THE LEGENDARY ORIGINS
OF THE TIANDIHUI

The Tiandihui, or "Heaven and Earth Society," was the most famous of the Chinese secret societies, and most present-day Chinese gangster groups, or "triads" trace their origin to it. There are various versions of a legend describing the Tiandihui's origins, one that is certainly far from the historical truth—the society was founded long after the burning of the monastery depicted, and did not originally have aspirations against the Qing emperors.[1] Nevertheless, the legend is the traditional, and widespread story about the secret society. The legend depicts an example of a blood-brotherhood formed among men who share an ambition to succeed at a very difficult long-term goal.

The story begins by detailing a tribe known as the Xi Lu rebels who in the 1670s plotted against Qing rule. The emperor Kangxi offers a reward to whoever can defeat them. This call is answered by the monks of the Shaolin Monastery. By their potent martial arts skills, they are able to put down the rebellion without losing any of their own men, even as the slain Xi Lu form a river of blood.

Amazed by their abilities, Emperor Kangxi begins to fear that the Shaolin monks are a threat. Treating them to a reward banquet at their monastery, he secretly has their drinks laced with sleep-inducing drugs, and that night, his men set fire to the building. A few of the monks wake up during the fire, and a way through the flames opens up for them after they pray, but the emperor's men kill most of them as they flee. Of the 128 monks at the Shaolin Monastery, only five escape Kangxi's treachery.

The five travel a great distance to be out of Kangxi's reach. They eventually reach the sea, where they are exhausted and must rest. They then see an incense-burner float to the surface of the water; at night it glows with the inscribed characters *Fan Qing Fu Ming*, "Overthrow the Ching, Restore the Ming." Overjoyed at this sign that Heaven wished them to have their revenge:

> "They then pricked their fingers, and mixing the
> blood with wine, drank it and swore an oath of
> brotherhood, pledging themselves to undertake
> this task, raise soldiers, buy horses, and collect all
> the braves of the Empire under their standard."[2]

Just after this, a teenage boy, with arms so long they reach to his knees, happens upon them, saying he wishes to join their forces. Asked why so young a man should think he could bring anything to the effort, he reveals his identity as the unknown grandson of Chongzhen, the last of the deposed Ming Emperors. The five monks are even more encouraged by this, and decide to further their mission by founding the secret Heaven and Earth Society, which gradually spreads throughout China and the world. The monks, Cai, Fang, Ma, Hu and Li, became known as "The Five Ancestors" among the Tiandihui.

FEI WEI AND CHI CH'ANG

The *Book of Lieh Tzu* is the third of the greatest Taoist philosophical writings, after the *Tao Te Ching* and the *Chuang Tzu*. It is traditionally attributed to a 5th century BCE philosopher Lieh Tzu, who was said to have been able to travel by riding the winds. However, modern scholars consider it to actually have been written in the third or fourth century CE. Among the many anecdotes compiled in the work is one concerning two archers, and the variety of blood-bond they make.[1]

Once in ancient times there was a great archer named Kan Ying. His skill was so profound that when he went out hunting, the beasts and the birds would only lay down passively, waiting for him to shoot them. Kan Ying gained a disciple, Fei Wei, who eventually gained even greater skill than his mentor. Fei Wei in turn had his own student, Chi Ch'ang.

Fei Wei told his student that before he could even presume to talk about archery, he must learn not to blink. Chi Ch'ang began to practice by lying down under his wife's loom, with his face below the pedal. After two years, he did not blink even when the sharp point came down right into the corner of his eye. Still the Master Fei Wei was not impressed.

"You must also learn how to see. You must see the small as the big, and the faint as the clear." Now Chi Ch'ang took up the challenge of staring at a flea which was suspended on the end of a hair, which he would gaze at from a great distance with the burning sun behind it. After years of this practice, the flea finally seemed to him as big as a cartwheel. In fact, everything Chi Ch'ang looked at, no matter how tiny or vague, was as plain to see as the hills and mountains. He then constructed an extremely fine arrow with a thorn for a head, and he proved able to shoot this through the flea's heart without breaking the hair.

Now Fei Wei jumped with glee at his student's success, and he went on teaching Chi Ch'ang until he had taught him all that he knew.

Not long after, Chi Ch'ang began to think of finding rivals to defeat. He gradually came to the realization that there was only one man that was even a worthy match for himself—Fei Wei. And so Chi Ch'ang planned to kill his teacher. The two met in the moorlands and prepared to shoot each other. When they both released their arrows, the arrowheads collided in mid-air, and fell uselessly to the ground. Fei Wei did not have another arrow, but when Chi Ch'ang sent another shot at him, he threw a bramble-thorn, which again hit Chi Ch'ang's arrow, with the same effect as before.

When they saw this, the two men broke out in tears, and threw away their bows. They bowed down low upon the ground before each other, and asked to become father and son. They both let blood flow from their arms, and took an oath never to reveal the secrets of their art to any other man.

While the story has little detail about the blood-ritual itself, presumably Fei Wei and Chi-Ch'ang mixed their blood in some way, rather than just releasing it. The story is primarily about masculine ambition to gain strength against both things, and other men. The resolution of the story is an example of the common theme of evenly matched rivals turning into allies; each sees a reflection of himself in the other. Since part of their vow is to keep their professional secrets, their blood-oath is something like those often used in initiations into secret societies and fraternities, but in this case, a society of only two men.

THE THREE SWORN BROTHERS

A CHINESE FOLKTALE

Practices of blood-brotherhood and sworn-brotherhood were common in the traditional culture of China. The motif of such brotherhoods often appears in Chinese folklore. One such folktale from the city of Shantou, in the Guangdong Province of southeastern China, concerns the life stories of three young boys.

Once there were three poor orphan boys who lived by begging. These three boys decided to become sworn-brothers, promising that if any one of them were become prosperous, he would share his wealth with the others. Sealing their vow, the three told their ages, and poured three handfuls of sand into one pile, and swore over this earth, and under Heaven, they would be one family. After this, they all slept under the same blanket, and cooked their food in the same pot. They all shared whatever little luck came to them.

After a few years, they thought to go separate ways to seek their fortunes, still agreeing that whoever was first to gain wealth or fame would notify the others. Then the three parted. The eldest and youngest of the brothers continued to live as beggars. The middle brother joined the army. He fought in a war against rebels on the frontier, and became promoted for bravery. He became a commandant, and his fame grew throughout China. After the war was over, he was appointed a province governor, and in this role he became widely known for his wise and competent rule.

Of course, the other two brothers also heard about his success, and they decided to go to the governor's palace to persuade him to fulfill the vow he had made so many years ago. They traveled until they were at the palace, and stood outside the gates. The elder brother decided he would go in to make the first appeal.

A trial was going on at that moment, and the eldest brother made a strange sight standing in front the spectators in his rags. He began addressing the governor, "I am your elder brother. When we were boys you looked to me for advice, and I always gave you half of what I had," and further recounted their past association. But the governor only signaled the officers of the court to seize the beggar. The elder brother shouted, "Don't you recognize your own sworn-brother?" but the governor only responded by ordering the officers to beat the vagabond, which they did quite happily. The elder brother was soon recounting tales of stolen chickens, and orchard raids, but only getting harder blows in return, until he was thrown out of the court building.

Outside, the elder brother warned the youngest brother about the governor's attitude, and told him that they had better flee, as their lives were in danger. The elder brother then went on, but the younger brother remained, and after some thought, entered the courtroom.

When the governor noticed his presence, the younger brother spoke to him deferentially. "You might well not remember me. We were brothers-in-arms during the war against the rebels many years ago. I was captured by the enemy in a foray and taken prisoner, but then you freed me from them by your own prowess. Because of that, even though I am poor, I wished to come the long way to pay my respects to you."

Everyone in the court was quite interested in this veteran, saved by their great governor himself. The governor smiled at him, and had new clothes brought for him, and a meal. Next the governor gave the veteran an office in the provincial government, sharing his power with his old brother-in-arms.[1]

THE FOUR SWORN BROTHERS

A KOREAN FOLKTALE

Rites of blood-brotherhood and other forms of sworn-brotherhood were once common to the traditional cultures of the Far East. References to these practices appear not only in some of the greater works of East Asian literature, but also can be found in popular folklore. One folktale of Korea involves an alliance of as many as four sworn-brothers. The story also has a motif common to Far East Asian folklore where a hero shows amazing strength even as a boy or baby. This retelling of the story is based on a version told by Zo Ze-ho, and collected by Zong In-sob.[1]

Once, a long, long time ago, there lived a man who unfortunately had no son. One day he found an abandoned baby boy which he took home and cared for. The boy grew in strength and intelligence incredibly fast. When he was only one month old, he asked his adopted father for a pack-carrier for him to bring firewood down from the mountains. The father made him one of straw, but the boy said it would not be strong enough. He also refused one made of wood, and only accepted one made of iron. Soon the father was surprised to see a mountain of lumber coming towards him—the little boy was hauling it all himself. The boy then built a new log home for the both of them, even finishing it with stone gate posts from rock that he had quarried on his own. The boy was so strong that he took to wearing footwear of iron, and so people began to call him Iron Shoes.

One day, Iron Shoes went on a journey. In a forest, he saw a very tall tree that was repeatedly falling down and standing up again by itself. He went closer and found a sleeping boy whose snoring breath was bending and releasing the tree. Iron Shoes tried to wake the boy, but he slept so soundly that Iron Shoes finally had to kick him in the nose to rouse him. He asked this young but mighty Nose Wind to become sworn-brothers with him, and he agreed. The two boys then wrestled, and as Nose Wind won the match, he was made the elder brother.

The two sworn-brothers went on their way together. One day they saw the strange sight of an entire mountain crumbling down swiftly into a level plain. They found a boy with a gigantic rake, who was working on the landscape. They asked him to become their sworn-brother, and he agreed. When Iron Shoes and Nose Wind sat on the handle of the rake, Long Rake was unable to lift it, and so the new boy became the youngest brother.

The three boys went on to seek adventure. One day they came to a great river that was running with brown water, despite the fact that there hadn't been any rain in recent days. They followed the river upstream to investigate, and found a boy who was urinating in a valley. When they grappled with him to test his might, they were nearly drowned in a torrent, and so Waterfall was made into the eldest sworn-brother.

After travelling many days, the four found a big house in the mountains with a tile roof. They knocked at the door, and an old woman with four sons answered. The sworn-brothers asked if they could have some food, and were warmly welcomed inside, and led to a large table in a room with stone walls and floor. A big supper was brought in to them, but the four sworn-brothers were dismayed to detect that all of the dishes were prepared from human flesh. They soon heard the dining room being locked from outside. The four only pretended to eat, and then pretended to go to sleep.

In the middle of the night, they overheard the old woman and her sons discussing how delicious their guests looked. Soon, the walls and the floor of the room began to grow hot. Nose Wind blew on them for the rest of the night to cool them off. In the morning, the old woman and the sons were surprised to find the brothers quite alive and uncooked, but both the wicked hosts and the guests kept acting as if nothing unusual were going on.

That same morning, the old woman suggested that the four sworn-brothers and her four sons have a woodcutting competition. The sworn-brothers would cut wood up on the mountain, and the sons would pile it up by the house. Whoever worked slower would be put to death.

The sworn-brothers tore up the trees whole by the roots, and threw them down the mountainside. The four wicked sons could hardly stack them so quickly. Sensing imminent defeat, the old woman had the two groups of boys switch places. Now the sworn-brothers were soon standing atop a great pile of lumber, idly waiting for the sons to send more down.

The old woman saw an opportunity in this. She set the pile of lumber on fire, and the four sworn-brothers were trapped on the top. The wicked family began clapping their hands in glee at the thought that their rivals would soon be well done.

But then, first sworn-brother Waterfall put out the fire, and also let loose a flood that had the vicious family submerged up to their necks, while the brothers stood safely far above. As they were nearly drowning, the old woman and the sons returned to their true form as man-eating tigers—just as the sworn brothers had suspected them to be. The vicious creatures began to beg for their lives.

But second sworn-brother Nose Wind sent out a breeze that froze the flood solid, and the five creatures were caught with just their heads and paws sticking out. Then third brother Iron Shoes began skating about on the ice, and his iron shoes neatly severed the tigers' appendages as he skated over them. Finally, fourth brother Long Rake broke up all the ice, and shoveled it off into a river, making the terrain just as it was before the whole calamity. The four sworn-brothers then all returned safely home.

Like many tales of sworn-brotherhood, the central theme of the story is males combining their strength for common goals and defense. Most practices of sworn-brotherhood superceded nature by making the "brothers" be as equals or peers regardless of their age; yet in this story, the boys replace age rank with rankings made after contesting of strength. In this way, a masculine value is used to replace the biological hierarchies of natural brotherhood with a hierarchy which the participants find preferable.

THE BALLAD OF EAST AND WEST
BY RUDYARD KIPLING (1889)

OH, East is East, and West is West,
and never the twain shall meet,
Till Earth and Sky stand presently
at God's great Judgment Seat;
But there is neither East nor West,
Border, nor Breed, nor Birth,
When two strong men stand face to face,
tho' they come from the ends of the earth!

Kamal is out with twenty men to raise the Border side,
And he has lifted the Colonel's mare
that is the Colonel's pride:
He has lifted her out of the stable-door
between the dawn and the day,
And turned the calkins upon her feet,
and ridden her far away.
Then up and spoke the Colonel's son
that led a troop of the Guides:
"Is there never a man of all my men
can say where Kamal hides?"
Then up and spoke Mahommed Khan,
the son of the Ressaldar,
"If ye know the track of the morning-mist,
ye know where his pickets are.
At dusk he harries the Abazai—
at dawn he is into Bonair,
But he must go by Fort Bukloh

to his own place to fare,
So if ye gallop to Fort Bukloh
as fast as a bird can fly,
By the favor of God ye may cut him off
ere he win to the Tongue of Jagai,
But if he be passed the Tongue of Jagai,
right swiftly turn ye then,
For the length and the breadth of that grisly
plain is sown with Kamal's men.
There is rock to the left, and rock to the right,
and low lean thorn between,
And ye may hear a breech-bolt snick
where never a man is seen."
The Colonel's son has taken a horse, and
a raw rough dun was he,
With the mouth of a bell and the heart of Hell,
and the head of the gallows-tree.
The Colonel's son to the Fort has won,
they bid him stay to eat—
Who rides at the tail of a Border thief,
he sits not long at his meat.
He 's up and away from Fort Bukloh
as fast as he can fly,
Till he was aware of his father's mare
in the gut of the Tongue of Jagai,
Till he was aware of his father's mare
with Kamal upon her back,
And when he could spy the white of her eye,
he made the pistol crack.
He has fired once, he has fired twice,
but the whistling ball went wide.
"Ye shoot like a soldier," Kamal said.
"Show now if ye can ride."
It 's up and over the Tongue of Jagai,
as blown dust-devils go,
The dun he fled like a stag of ten,
but the mare like a barren doe.
The dun he leaned against the bit and slugged
his head above,

But the red mare played with the snaffle-bars,
as a maiden plays with a glove.
There was rock to the left and rock to the right,
and low lean thorn between,
And thrice he heard a breech-bolt snick tho' never
a man was seen.
They have ridden the low moon out of the sky,
their hoofs drum up the dawn,
The dun he went like a wounded bull,
but the mare like a new-roused fawn.
The dun he fell at a water-course—
in a woful heap fell he,
And Kamal has turned the red mare back,
and pulled the rider free.
He has knocked the pistol out of his hand—small
room was there to strive,
"'T was only by favor of mine," quoth
he, "ye rode so long alive:
There was not a rock for twenty mile, there
was not a clump of tree,
But covered a man of my own men
with his rifle cocked on his knee.
If I had raised my bridle-hand,
as I have held it low,
The little jackals that flee so fast,
were feasting all in a row:
If I had bowed my head on my breast,
as I have held it high,
The kite that whistles above us now were gorged till
she could not fly."
Lightly answered the Colonel's son:—"Do good
to bird and beast,
But count who come for the broken meats
before thou makest a feast.
If there should follow a thousand swords
to carry my bones away,
Belike the price of a jackal's meal
were more than a thief could pay.
They will feed their horse on the standing crop,

their men on the garnered grain,
The thatch of the byres will serve their
fires when all the cattle are slain.
But if thou thinkest the price be fair—
thy brethren wait to sup,
The hound is kin to the jackal-spawn—howl, dog,
and call them up!
And if thou thinkest the price be high, in
steer and gear and stack,
Give me my father's mare again,
and I'll fight my own way back!"
Kamal has gripped him by the hand
and set him upon his feet.
"No talk shall be of dogs," said he,
"when wolf and gray wolf meet.
May I eat dirt if thou hast hurt of me in deed or breath;
What dam of lances brought thee forth
to jest at the dawn with Death?"
Lightly answered the Colonel's son:
"I hold by the blood of my clan:
Take up the mare for my father's gift—
by God, she has carried a man!"
The red mare ran to the Colonel's son,
and nuzzled against his breast,
"We be two strong men," said Kamal then,
"but she loveth the younger best.
So she shall go with a lifter's dower, my
turquoise-studded rein,
My broidered saddle and saddle-cloth,
and silver stirrups twain."
The Colonel's son a pistol drew and held it muzzle-end,
"Ye have taken the one from a foe," said he;
"will ye take the mate from a friend?"
"A gift for a gift," said Kamal straight;
"a limb for the risk of a limb.
Thy father has sent his son to me,
I'll send my son to him!"
With that he whistled his only son,
that dropped from a mountain-crest—

He trod the ling like a buck in spring, and he
looked like a lance in rest.
"Now here is thy master," Kamal said,
"who leads a troop of the Guides,
And thou must ride at his left side as
shield on shoulder rides.
Till Death or I cut loose the tie,
at camp and board and bed,
Thy life is his—thy fate it is
to guard him with thy head.
So thou must eat the White Queen's meat,
and all her foes are thine,
And thou must harry thy father's hold
for the peace of the border-line.
And thou must make a trooper tough and
hack thy way to power—
Belike they will raise thee to Ressaldar
when I am hanged in Peshawur."

They have looked each other between the eyes,
and there they found no fault,
They have taken the Oath of the Brother-in Blood
on leavened bread and salt:
They have taken the Oath of the Brother-in-Blood
on fire and fresh-cut sod,
On the hilt and the haft of the Khyber knife,
and the Wondrous Names of God.

The Colonel's son he rides the mare
and Kamal's boy the dun,
And two have come back to Fort Bukloh
where there went forth but one.
And when they drew to the Quarter-Guard,
full twenty swords flew clear—
There was not a man but carried his feud with the
blood of the mountaineer.
"Ha' done! ha' done!" said the Colonel's son.
"Put up the steel at your sides!
Last night ye had struck at a Border thief—to-

night 't is a man of the Guides!"

Oh, East is East, and West is West, and
never the two shall meet,
Till Earth and Sky stand presently at
God's great Judgment Seat;
But there is neither East nor West,
Border, nor Breed, nor Birth,
When two strong men stand face to face,
tho' they come from the ends of the earth.

THE TATENOKAI BLOOD OATH

Following the release of his novel *Confessions of a Mask* in 1948, Yukio Mishima became one of the most celebrated authors and playwrights in modern Japanese history. He was nominated for the Nobel Prize in literature in the 1960s and his novels, as well as his impressive catalog of plays, short stories and essays are still widely read and have been translated into several languages. Mishima's novels often dealt with tragic themes, including suicide and death.

As his fame grew, Mishima became obsessed with his own masculinity and self-image. He saw himself as a sickly intellectual dandy whose body and spirit had been corrupted by his lifelong obsession with words. In the 1950s, he began bodybuilding, and committed himself to becoming a man not only of words, but of action—to become a man of both the pen and the sword. To this end, not only did he successfully reshape his body, but he also achieved 5th dan status as a Kendo master, and starred as a street thug in the *yakuza* film "Afraid to Die." His precise reasons for undergoing this personal transformation are detailed in his autobiographical manifesto, *Sun & Steel*.[1]

Another manifestation of this change in Mishima was his distinctive brand of right-wing nationalism which was primarily focused on loyalty to the *idea* of the Emperor as a symbol of authentic Japanese culture, values and spirit. In 1967, he enlisted in the Ground Self Defense Force (GSDF), and underwent basic training. Soon thereafter, he formed his own paramilitary organization, known as the *Tatenokai*, or "Shield Society," devoted to protecting the Emperor. Because of his celebrity status and because he maintained a friendly relationship with the GSDF, Mishima was permitted to use military facilities to train members of the *Tatenokai*.

In the early days of the *Tatenokai*, Mishima met with some young men at the offices of the *Ronso Journal*, a right-wing magazine produced by college students. He pulled out a piece of paper and wrote, "We hereby swear to be the foundation of Imperial Japan." Then he cut his finger and dripped his blood into a cup, and the young men followed suit. Each man signed his name on the piece of paper, using the collective blood of the group. Then Mishima decided that they should all drink the remaining blood, and asked jokingly if anyone present had a venereal disease. As he surveyed the room full of men with blood on their mouths and teeth, he said, "What a fine lot of Draculas," and laughed. [2]

Real life and fiction then overlapped in Mishima's 1969 novel *Runaway Horses*, which tells the tale of a group of ultra-nationalist students who, inspired by the book *The League of the Divine Wind*, plot to assassinate corrupt national leaders and businessmen, and then commit *seppuku*, a ritual suicide, also known as *hara-kiri*. In *Runaway Horses*, the members of the "Showa League of the Divine Wind" meet at a Shinto temple to purify themselves, recite their vows and seal their alliance under the stars and in the presence of the gods. The final vow was:

> "Be it thus that we, never seeking power and giving no thought to personal advancement, go forth to certain death to become the foundation stones for the Restoration."

Immediately afterwards, the characters reached out to clasp each others hands.

"Grasping hands were everywhere as though a growth of tenacious ivy had sprung up from the darkness. Each tendril, whether sweaty of dry or hard or soft to the touch, was filled with strength as it held fast for a brief moment marked by a mutual sharing of the warmth of their bodies and their blood. Isao dreamed that he would some night stand like this with his comrades upon the field of battle, taking wordless farewell before their deaths."[3]

On November 25, 1970, Yukio Mishima and four members of the *Tatenokai* visited the Tokyo headquarters of Japan's military and took one of their contacts, General Mashita, hostage in his own office. They were armed only with bladed weapons. One of these was Mishima's 16th century samurai sword. Mishima and his men fought with a few members of the military who tried to stop them. Barred in Mashita's office, they demanded that the troops be summoned to hear Mishima make a patriotic speech from a nearby rooftop. After shouting at a crowd of jeering, disrespectful soldiers, Mishima returned to Mashita's office, and committed ritual *seppuku*. In the traditional manner, he was beheaded by his closest comrade, Masakatsu Morita who then followed him to his death.

AUSTRALIA AND THE PACIFIC ISLANDS

A variety of blood-rituals existed in the aboriginal cultures of Australia and many islands of the western Pacific, especially the diverse region of the Malay Archipelago. There are many examples from this region of the world, and this chapter will only include some of the most interesting of them. These ceremonies were still in practice when European travelers were making their initial contacts with the region, so that many explorers and missionaries were able to make observations of the rites, and often took part in them themselves.

Among the Arrernte people of central Australia young men sometimes gave their blood to older men, with the belief that this would give strength to the latter. Men's blood was similarly used in a vengeance expedition, or *atninga*. The older men of the group would select one of the party to give the blood, and the others would then both drink the blood and have it spurted onto their bodies, which was thought to make them more strong, lithe, and active in preparation for their mission. Furthermore, this use of the blood was thought to prevent any treachery against the group's plans; a man who drank the blood was bound not to warn any of his friends even if it was their locality that was to be attacked. This binding power of the blood was thought to be effective whether the drinking had been voluntary or not.[1]

A blood-brotherhood relationship known as *poining gumbar* existed among the now-extinct Wiilman tribe and neighboring peoples of southwestern Australia. The creation of the bond between two men of different tribes was often used to signify adoption of one man by the other's tribe. The bond was considered to be closer than that between ordinary kin, because of its voluntary nature, and even closer than the bond between spouses. The creation of matching scars upon the men might serve as an identifying mark of the *poining gumbar* relationship.[2]

In an initiation ceremony of the aborigines of New South Wales, it was the custom of the initiate to drink the blood of his companions, thus securing a union between himself and the clan.[3]

Blood rituals existed on several of the Sunda Islands, especially Borneo. A form of the blood pact involving *smoking* the blood was used by Borneo's nomadic Penan people, particularly when making alliances with the settled Kayan and Kenyah. Two men sat facing each other, and one made a cut on the front of his left shoulder, and smeared the blood on a cigarette, and gave it to the other to smoke; the second man did the same. Henceforth they called each other *sabilah*, or "friend." It was believed that if either man (or even any member of the group he represented) were to violate the pact, then he would automatically meet his death by vomiting of blood. The pact involved assurance of safety from attack, and promises of vengeance against attacking third parties.[4]

A similar ritual in Borneo had the two men combining their blood into a single cigarette, which they then took turns smoking. Afterwards, a fowl was sacrificed, and the gods called to witness the men's promise to treat each other as brothers and always to help one another, and even if facing starvation to "share the last grain of rice."[5]

Among the Dusun people of Borneo, a blood-brotherhood rite involved each man sucking a blood from a cut of the other's wrist, followed by an exchange of gifts. Sometimes a fowl was also sacrificed, each man swearing, "If I cheat you, may I become as this fowl which has just been killed."[6]

Another example of a blood pact of Borneo was one made between two Dayak rulers and two Christian missionaries. Two officers used small knives to take some blood from the arm of each of the four men, and the blood was mixed into four separate glasses of water. Each man then drank from the glasses of the others, after which they joined hands and kissed. The two Dayak chieftains then declared, "Brethren, be not afraid to dwell with us, for we will do you no harm; and if others wish to hurt you, we will defend you with our life's blood, and die ourselves ere you be slain."[7]

A ceremony of blood-brotherhood as a swearing of eternal friendship, and involving *planting a tree* existed on the island of Timor of the Lesser Sundas. The ritual could have been performed between individuals or between groups. The contracting parties slashed their arms, and mixed the blood into a bamboo container. The container was taken to a secluded location along with a small fig tree, a ritual spear and a sword. The tree was then planted, with the weapons flanking it, and the bamboo container was hung upon it. The two parties then drank the mixed blood with gin, leaving some in the container. Each then swore "If I be false, and not a true friend, may blood issue from my mouth, ears, and nose as it does from this bamboo,"—and at that moment the receptacle was pricked to allow the mixed blood and gin to pour out upon the tree. The tree was left to grow there as the "witness" of the oath. This Timorese blood-brotherhood was a very strong bond; each man was considered to be perfectly free in the other's home, and nothing one would ask from the other was denied. One would even give access to his wife to the other, and if a child was born from this, the actual husband would regard the child as his own.[8]

Among the Rokka people of the Sunda island of Flores, friendship was sealed by a blood ritual, wherein the participants reciprocally sucked blood from a wound made in the other's hand. This ritual was performed in honor of the god Atagai.[9]

Blood-bond rituals were also practiced on several of the Maluku islands (once known as the Spice Islands). On Seram, it was used in settling conflicts between two villages, and ratifying peace after a war. One village had a great feast to which the other village was invited. A single dish of food was placed before both of the chiefs of both parties. The chiefs' blood was added to this dish, and also a sword and other weapons dipped into it, and the chiefs ate from it one after the other. After this, the second village put on a feast identical in all ways with the first, sealing the bond.[10] On the Babar islands, a blood-ritual was used to make peace between two villages or a league of friendship between two individuals. The two parties drank liquor with blood from the both of them mixed into it.[11] Drinking blood also sealed a bond between either villages or individuals on Wetar. Somewhat like kinship, members of the villages involved in such a bond could not intermarry. [12]

A blood-oath tradition existed among the Papuans of the island on New-Guinea. Both parties would cut both of their arms with a sharp bamboo, and then suck each other's blood from the wounds. This constituted a promise to do each other no mischief.[13] This Papuan oath also seems to have entailed obligations and rights similar to actual kinship; once, when a missionary working in New Guinea died, his native "blood friends" came to take possession of all of his property, and divided it up among themselves—much to the astonishment of the fellow missionaries, who were not familiar with the custom.[14]

A blood-brotherhood ceremony existed among the aboriginal people of Taiwan. Two friends would pour wine into a goblet, and after mixing it with their blood, would drink from it at the same time.[15]

Blood-rituals were also found in several of the Philippine islands. Ferdinand Magellan was the first Western explorer to reach the Philippines amid his famous 1519 journey to find a westward passage to the East Indies, and he and his followers met with several examples of such traditions. At an island which Magellan called Mazaba or Mazaua (historians are in dispute about its location), Magellan exchanged several gifts with a local king, who then expressed the wish that he and the explorer become *casi casi*. The two then tasted a few drops of each other's blood, after which they were considered "brothers" by the local custom.[16] Another example of blood-brotherhood was to be found on the island of Cebu. While Magellan was in his ship, docked on the shore, the king of Cebu had a drop of blood from his right arm sent to Magellan, with a request that he do the same, which Magellan did.[17]

After Magellan's death in the Battle of Mactan near Cebu in 1521, his followers continued the voyage, and encountered more blood rituals on other Philippine islands. At Mindanao, a king made a demonstration of peace by taking blood from his left hand, and smearing it on his own face, tongue, and body, as an expression of greatest friendship. The men of the Spanish ships did likewise.[18] A very similar rite was found at Palawan, the local king smearing blood from his chest onto his tongue and forehead as a sign of truest peace, with the European travelers reciprocating.[19]

A famous historical blood-pact occurred on the Philippine island of Bohol, in 1565 involving the Rajah Sikatuna of that island, and the Spanish explorer and conquistador Miquel Lopez de Legazpi. Each man made a cut upon his chest or arm, and drank the blood of the other mixed with wine or water. This custom was regarded as the most sacred bond of friendship.[20] This event, known as the *Sandugo*, is celebrated in an annual Sandugo Festival, and the blood ceremony is even represented on both the flag and the seal of Bohol Province.

A rather late occurrence of a blood-compact among the Philippines was its use by the *Katipunan*, a secret society founded in 1892, which sought Philippine independence from Spain and did much to bring about the Philippine Revolution of 1896–1898. Members of the secret league would have blood drown from a cut on the leg or arm, and would then use the blood to sign their name of the roll of fraternity. The scar from the cut was also a secret mark by which members of the league could recognize each other.[21]

THE NAME EXCHANGE

JACK LONDON'S "THE HEATHEN"

While this book has so far been concerned primarily with blood-oaths, blood-brotherhood, and other forms of created brotherhood, this chapter will discuss another rite of alliance, known to anthropology as "name-exchange." In this practice, two men would actually give their names to each other, afterward calling each other by the name that was previously their own. Often, other people would call the men by their new names as well. This ritual of name-swapping sometimes accompanied blood-brotherhood rituals[1], and at times customarily led to a pretend-hostile "joking relationship."[2]

The name-exchange custom was especially prominent in the region of Oceania. On the island of Mabuiag, in the Torres Strait between Australia and New Guinea, the ceremony of trading names between friends was known as *natam*.[3] A man might thus swap names with various men several times in his life, and in an advanced version of the ritual, some men might go so far as to have even their wives and children exchange names at the same time.[4] In San Cristoval in the Solomon Islands, men whose friendships were recognized by the swapping of names were known as *marahu*. Such men were thought to have rights to one another's properties, and as with an adoption, they would appropriately change their terms of address for each other's kin as well.[5] In Polynesia, as a manner of formally recognizing friendship, the rite of name exchanging was practiced in Tahiti, where it may have been as important to the networks of Tahitian kinship as marriage.[6]

The name-swapping practice of *hakahoa* was often used as a sign of hospitality between a host and his guest in the Marquesan Islands.[7] The ritual also could confer a full sharing of property rights.[8] When Captain David Porter swapped names with a Marquesan native, he was surprised to find the new "Tavee" soon offering the captain his wife.[9]

There is evidence of the name-swapping ritual reaching to the other side of the Pacific, among indigenous North Americans. In his famous circumnavigation of the globe, Sir Francis Drake landed at North America, possibly in the region of northern California. There his party was met by many natives and their chieftain, called "Hioh." After an elaborate ceremony with dancing, singing, and speeches, this chieftain placed a headdress and ornamental chains upon Drake, and began referring to him as "Hioh."[10] Drake thought that this meant that he was being made into a chief himself, but anthropologists suggest that a name-exchange was used politically as a statement of peace.

The origins of the practice of name-exchange are unknown, but the custom seems to involve a certain folk-magic logic. A person's name was often considered to be a part or aspect *of their soul.* As such, there have often been practices of keeping one's name secret from those who might misuse it to work mischief, and of making a formal event out of revealing names. [11] Taking this one step further, swapping names was a way of exchanging a piece of one's innermost being with another.

In this respect, the name-exchange is thematically similar to blood-brotherhood practices, as blood was often considered to be a soul-substance. Even for a modern man without such a literal belief in the power of names, the practice could be a profound expression of a bond, as people still have a strong psychological identification with their names. Such a feeling might have been involved in the many instances of men from the West swapping names with native men of the South Pacific.

Such an exchange is the subject of Jack London's "The Heathen." In this short story, London tells of two men from different cultures who are shipwrecked together after a hurricane sinks their overloaded schooner, and of the rewarding lifelong bond they form as a result of that experience. The main characters are Charley, an American seeking his fortune, and Otoo, who is described as a "black kanaka heathen" from Bora Bora.

The exchange of names in "The Heathen" is largely symbolic and private. Neither man uses the other's name in everyday life. Otoo says simply, "Whenever I think of myself, I shall think of you." The name trade itself remains something that matters only to the two men, though the closeness of their seventeen year friendship is evident to all who meet them. London alludes to name exchange happening only at the moment of greatest meaning, i.e. "beyond the sky and beyond the stars."

The excerpt below begins by recounting the decision to exchange names while the men await rescue, and ends with some poignant passages conveying the potential for one man's steady devotion to influence another man's behavior in a positive way.

From Jack London's
"The Heathen" (1909)

In the end, Otoo saved my life; for I came to lying on the beach twenty feet from the water, sheltered from the sun by a couple of cocoanut leaves. No one but Otoo could have dragged me there and stuck up the leaves for shade. He was lying beside me. I went off again; and the next time I came round, it was [a] cool and starry night, and Otoo was pressing a drinking cocoanut to my lips.

We were the sole survivors of the Petite Jeanne. Captain Oudouse must have succumbed to exhaustion, for several days later his hatch cover

drifted ashore without him. Otoo and I lived with
the natives of the atoll for a week, when we were
rescued by the French cruiser and taken to Tahiti.
In the meantime, however, we had performed the
ceremony of exchanging names. In the South Seas
such a ceremony binds two men closer together than
blood brothership. The initiative had been mine; and
Otoo was rapturously delighted when I suggested it.

"It is well," he said, in Tahitian. "For we have been
mates together for two days on the lips of Death."

"But death stuttered," I smiled.

"It was a brave deed you did, master," he replied,
"and Death was not vile enough to speak."

"Why do you 'master' me?" I demanded, with a
show of hurt feelings. "We have exchanged names.
To you I am Otoo. To me you are Charley. And
between you and me, forever and forever, you shall
be Charley, and I shall be Otoo. It is the way of the
custom. And when we die, if it does happen that we
live again somewhere beyond the stars and the sky,
still shall you be Charley to me, and I Otoo to you."

"Yes, master," he answered, his eyes luminous and
soft with joy.

"There you go!" I cried indignantly.

"What does it matter what my lips utter?" he argued.
"They are only my lips. But I shall think Otoo
always. Whenever I think of myself, I shall think of
you. Whenever men call me by name, I shall think
of you. And beyond the sky and beyond the stars,
always and forever, you shall be Otoo to me. Is it
well, master?"

I hid my smile, and answered that it was well.

We parted at Papeete. I remained ashore to recuperate; and he went on in a cutter to his own island, Bora Bora. Six weeks later he was back. I was surprised, for he had told me of his wife, and said that he was returning to her, and would give over sailing on far voyages.

"Where do you go, master?" he asked, after our first greetings.

I shrugged my shoulders. It was a hard question.

"All the world," was my answer—"all the world, all the sea, and all the islands that are in the sea."

"I will go with you," he said simply. "My wife is dead."

I never had a brother; but from what I have seen of other men's brothers, I doubt if any man ever had a brother that was to him what Otoo was to me. He was brother and father and mother as well. And this I know: I lived a straighter and better man because of Otoo. I cared little for other men, but I had to live straight in Otoo's eyes. Because of him I dared not tarnish myself. He made me his ideal, compounding me, I fear, chiefly out of his own love and worship and there were times when I stood close to the steep pitch of hell, and would have taken the plunge had not the thought of Otoo restrained me. His pride in me entered into me, until it became one of the major rules in my personal code to do nothing that would diminish that pride of his.

THE AMERICAS

A widespread impression among many Americans and Europeans, spread through many movies and novels, is that blood-brotherhood was a common practice among Native Americans. This is something of a myth. Blood-brotherhood has been primarily an Old World phenomenon, and evidence of the practice among the aboriginal peoples of the New World is scanty. However, there have been several instances of highly similar cultural items, such as created brotherhood, blood-rites, and blood-brotherhood-like ideas in some of their religious myths.

A kind of created brotherhood existed among the Plains Cree of Canada's Prairie Provinces. Two boys would become great friends, sharing the risks of the warpath. The relationship commenced with one leaving his family to stay with the clan of the other for a time. Each would refer to the other's parents as their own mother and father; when the two got married, their wives would refer to each other by in a similar manner. If one of the boys were to die in childhood, the surviving one would go to live with the deceased's family for a period of time, and then after this both households were considered equally his own. All this is like the common pattern of blood-brotherhood across cultures, but this relationship was not marked by any formal ceremony. The term by which each called the other was *niwitcewahakun*, meaning simply "he with whom I go about."[1]

A blood-rite was used among the Coast Pomo Indians of Northern California in the initiations of boys into the adults' secret society. The ceremony was attended by a neophyte, a relative whose position in the society the neophyte would take, and an initiator, or *yomta*. First, the boy would take an oath to keep the secrets of the society, and to recognize various taboos, pertaining to such things as sacred animals, and to sexuality. The initiator then rubbed the youth's body with herbs. Lastly, either the yomta or the relative scratched the initiate's arm and transferred the blood to the relative. [2]

Among the Zacatecos of Central Mexico a ceremony similar to blood-brotherhood was used when one tribe wished to form a close connection or alliance with another. One tribe took a man from the other tribe, and he was to be the focus of the ritual. He was made to fast for a whole day, while all the others had a feast. At the end of the fast, the man was plied with a great quantity of alcohol, and then his ears were pierced several times with a deer-bone awl. His blood was then used to anoint the members of the opposite tribe.[3]

A simple blood custom existed among the indigenous population of the Yucatan peninsula. When new friends were received, as a token of the establishment of the friendship, each friend would draw a bit of blood from their hand, arm, tongue, or another part of the body in the sight of the other.[4]

In Central America, a notion similar to blood-brotherhood figured in the religious traditions of the Miskito people of the Atlantic coast of Nicaragua and Honduras. The Miskitos thought that prior to important undertakings, it was beneficial to have the help of a *nagual*, a kind of guardian spirit. This spirit was thought to have the form of an animal or bird. In order to make contact with the nagual, a seeker would offer up a sacrifice in a secluded location. When the nagual appeared—perhaps in some sort of dream or vision—blood was drawn from several parts of the body, to seal the compact for life. The man and the spirit were thought to become so closely linked together in fate, that if either one were to die, the other would as well.[5]

In South America, a variety of blood-brotherhood practice existed among the Yekuána and Guaica peoples of the Orinico River region of Venezuela, used whenever a war-party of men was on their way to meet their enemy. The ritual was intended to ensure solidarity; noone was allowed to turn away from the fight once the rite was done. In the ritual, two leaders of the party cut themselves on their arms, and poured some of their blood into the nose of the other, using a simple funnel made from a leaf. They then refer to each other as *wuéčakono*, which means "my intimate one," and which is also the same term used between natural brothers who love each other greatly.[6]

The Tupi people of Brazil practiced a variety of created brotherhood. Calling each other *atourassap*, the bond signified men who loved each other as much as natural brothers. The bond also was considered as sacred as true brotherhood; neither man could marry the daughters or sisters of the other. They also held all possessions in common.[7]

A blood-brotherhood oath called *konchotun* existed in the culture of the indigenous Mapuche people, of central and southern Chile and southern Argentina. A sacrificial sheep was used, and its right ear severed. The men swore mutual aid and lifelong friendship over the animal's blood. This ritual was sometimes performed amid the complex *ñillatun* fertility rite, which was itself centered on the sacrificial use of a sheep's blood and heart.[8]

Blood-brotherhood also figured in the totemistic concepts of the Mapuche, as well as some other Andean peoples. Each clan identified itself with a totem animal or bird, or some other living thing, or else with some non-living natural phenomenon, such as a celestial body, which was in turn represented by a living thing. In either case, the creature was referred to as the "brother" of the clan, and members of the clan would also identify themselves as its "children." Some of the clans explained this relationship as caused by a literal descent from the animal, sometimes by a myth of a human woman mating with the creature and founding the clan. But more often, the mythical explanation was of a male ancestor having formed a blood-pact with the animal, the man taking on the creature's name, and thus both promising mutual protection to each other and all of their descendants.[9]

MASHTINNA

Contrary to many popular ideas, customs of blood-brotherhood were not common to Native North American peoples. Notwithstanding, there were some customs of brother-making, as well as other ways by which men recognized friends of particular distinction. One folktale of the Dakota Sioux involves two men who are comrades or "brother-friends."[1]

Once there was a young man called Mashtinna, which meant "Rabbit." He was very handsome, and also generous, to a fault. One day while he was hunting in the woods, he heard the alarming cries of a child in the distance. He rushed to find the child. On the far side of the woods, he saw a person pinching and striking a baby boy. This person was singing a sweet lullaby as he did so, and was only laughing and smiling.

"Why are you abusing this innocent child?" Mashtinna demanded, but the stranger only smiled and replied in a pleasant tone, "What are you talking about? This baby is fretful, and I'm just trying to soothe him."

Mashtinna thought then that this person was the Double-Face, a creature that had always enjoyed tormenting the helpless. "Give the boy to me!" Mashtinna demanded. The stranger then flipped the other side of its face forward, which was dark and scowling. "Say another word, and I'll treat you the same," it threatened.

Mashtinna then loaded his bow, and shot the Double-Face straight through the heart.

Mashtinna then took up the little child in his arms, and thought about how to find his family. He followed a nearby trail that lead to a single small teepee. He looked inside, and found an old man and woman, both blind. "Hello, grandfather and grandmother," he said, "I've brought back for you the baby you lost!" But the couple shouted back "Ugh, no, you trickster! You've already taken away everyone we had! We won't believe a thing you say! Get away!"

Seeing that these people had been too terrorized by the Double-Face to trust anyone at all, and that they wouldn't even take the child, Mashtinna knew that he would have to care for the little one himself. Night was falling, and so he wrapped the baby boy up in his own cloth and went to sleep.

The next morning, Mashtinna was astonished to see that the baby had grown in the night, and was now a young man like himself. He even looked like Mashtinna, so much so that the two might have been twins.

"My friend, we are comrades for life," the strange youth declared. "We will go separate ways in the world, and we will do different good deeds, but if either of us is in trouble, he needs only to call for help and the other will come instantly." Mashtinna agreed with all this, and so the two men went off in different directions.

Not long after this, as Mashtinna was traveling through the woods, he heard a sound like a man crying and groaning in great pain. When he followed the sound, he saw a great forked tree, with the man stuck in the crevices of the branches. As the wind blew, the tree moved and pinched the man terribly. He was in great misery, and could not get away.

"I will take your place!" Mashtinna declared, and the tree opened up, releasing the man and taking in Mashtinna. The tree pinched him like a vise, and the pain was much worse than he had thought. He bore the agony for as long as he could, the sweat breaking on his brow, and veins bulging on his forehead. Finally he could take no more, and called out to his comrade for help. His brother-friend appeared instantly, and struck the tree so that it opened up and let Mashtinna free.

Mashtinna then continued on his travels, and after a time came to a lone small wigwam at the wood's edge. Its single inhabitant was a poor old blind man. The man was happy to have a visitor. The blind man explained to Mashtinna how he managed. "This long strip of rawhide leads me to the stream, and this rope leads around the woods. I've got plenty of pemmican in these bags. So I can live, but how piteous to live blind and alone!"

Mashtinna wanted to help this man, and so he gave him his eyes. The old man then went off into the world, while Mashtinna took up his place. He found that the store of dried meat satisfied his hunger, but also made him thirsty. He felt along the rawhide rope to get to the stream, but just as he was stooping over the stream at the bank, the rope broke, and Mashtinna fell in the water. With some struggle, he found his way out of the stream, but now he was very cold, and knew he would need to go into the woods to get firewood.

He took hold of the other rope, and felt his way in and out of the woods for a while, but eventually he lost track of the rope, and became confused as to where he was. Soon he was tripping over the logs, bumping himself on the trees, and scratching himself on the briars. It began to seem he could take no more, and so he called out to his comrade for help.

As before, his brother-friend appeared instantly and gave him back his eyes. But he also admonished him at the same time, "You shouldn't be so rash in the future! It's fine to help others, but you should consider whether you yourself can endure something or not."

The basic lesson of the story is the importance of a man knowing the limitations of his own strength. The bond between Mashtinna and his friend is after a pattern common to many cultural traditions of sworn-brotherhood, where the men promise each other important mutual assistance, whether they expect to be in each other's company for much time or little. Mashtinna's brother-friend is portrayed like an ideal fantasy◉looking like his twin and making magical sudden appearances. But there is also an important element of realism, as Mashtinna must listen to his comrade's blunt criticism.

WINNETOU & OLD SHATTERHAND

Karl May (1842-1912) is one of the best selling German authors of all time. His travel and adventure stories have been translated into over 30 European languages, but they remain especially popular with Germans, a million of whom attend the Karl May Festival held in Bad Segeburg, Germany every summer. Albert Einstein, Adolf Hitler, Hermann Hesse, Fritz Lang, Franz Josef Strauss, Thomas Mann and Arnold Schwarzenegger are just a few of the notable figures who have expressed an affinity for his work at one time or another.

Winnetou I, the first in a series of novels featuring the blood-brothers Winnetou, an Apache, and Old Shatterhand, an adventure-seeking German immigrant to America's Wild West, is May's most popular novel. The characters have been featured in several German-language films, and are as well known to Germans as Tonto and The Lone Ranger are to Americans. However, May's Wild West stories never really caught on with Americans, probably because they are particularly German. As scholar Richard H. Cracroft wrote in his introduction to an English translation of *Winnetou*, Karl May's characters drink German beer, read German newspapers, and sing German songs. Old Shatterhand, May's hero and alter ego, "symbolizes May's estimation of the ideal virtues of late 19th century Germany." Indeed, the villains in Old Shatterhand's saga are often greedy or immoral Americans, who are corrected or brought to justice by the noble German. May was influenced by American writers like James Fenimore Cooper and Longfellow, and undoubtedly studied the American

West from afar, but he only visited the United States once, many years after he had become famous for writing about it. As such, his depiction of the blood-brotherhood rite of the Apaches should not be read as an authentic portrayal grounded in historical fact, but an appealing fantasy that has moved and inspired generations of German readers.

The story begins as Charlie, a "greenhorn" fresh off the boat from Germany, is adopted by experienced "Westerner" Sam Hawkins, who takes him on an expedition to survey land for a rail line and attempts to teach him the ways of the West. Charlie gets his nickname, Old Shatterhand, from Sam, who observes his remarkable strength, courage and his ability to knock a man out with one punch. Though it is Sam who is the acknowledged "Westerner," the impossibly well-read and nearly superhuman Old Shatterhand makes him look like a fumbling novice during virtually every "lesson" — from shooting Buffalo to breaking wild horses and, finally, killing a furious grizzly with a Bowie knife.

It is in the process of defeating the grizzly that Old Shatterhand is first observed by Winnetou. Winnetou intervenes on Old Shatterhand's behalf during a dispute with ne'er-do-well Rattler, a member of the surveying party who mocks Charlie and attempts to lay claim to the bear even though he retreated to the trees as Charlie fought courageously.

> "Uff! The squirrels and skunks are such, to flee up the trees when a foe draws near. But a man should fight, for if he possesses courage, then the power is given him to overcome the strongest beast himself. My young white brother had such courage. Why is he called a greenhorn?"

Winnetou and Old Shatterhand share a quiet mutual respect that is brief, as Winnetou's father, High Chief of the Mescalero Apaches, soon discovers that the group is being paid to measure Apache territory for a "firehorse" sure to bring thieving and killing white men. As the dispute becomes heated, the drunken

Rattler shoots and kills the Winnetou's beloved tutor, a white man-turned-Apache named Kleki-Petrah. The Apaches swear to avenge Kleki-Petrah's death and return to Old Shatterhand's camp with an army of braves.

What follows is a complex series of events whereby Old Shatterhand and Sam Hawkins scheme to both save their surveying party and redeem themselves in the eyes of the Apaches. Old Shatterhand's complex and risky strategy involves a battle between the Kiowas and the Apaches, wherein he secretly saves Winnetou's life after Winnetou and his father are taken prisoner by the Kiowas. Injured in battle, and unable to speak or defend himself, Old Shatterhand is taken prisoner by the Apaches and sentenced to be tortured to death along with his white associates as soon as he has regained his former strength. At his trial, he attempts to plead his case, and is offered a chance to prove his innocence and worthiness by winning a seemingly impossible challenge. When he succeeds through the use of cunning, he wins his freedom and reveals evidence of his noble intentions. After this redemption, he is embraced by the Apaches and by Winnetou, and the two are finally able to discuss the circumstances surrounding the death of Winnetou's white mentor, Kleki-Petrah.

[Old Shatterhand] "He asked me to remain true to you."

[Winnetou] "Remain true to me? You did not even know me yet."

"I knew you, for I had seen you, and whoever sees Winnetou knows who he has before him, and he had told me about you."

"What answer did you give him?"

"I promised to fulfill his wish."

"It was the last that he had in his life. You have become his heir. You vowed to him to be true to me, protected, guarded, and looked after me, while I pursued you as an enemy. My knife-stroke would have been deadly to any other, but your strong body overcame it. I stand in deep, deep debt to you. Be my friend!"

"I have already long been that."

"My brother!"

"With all my heart, gladly."

"Then we will seal the bond at the grave of him who handed over my soul to you! One noble paleface has gone from us, and even in death has sent us another just as noble. My blood shall be your blood and your blood shall be mine! I will drink yours, and you will drink mine. Intschu-Tschuna, the greatest chief of the Apache, my father and begetter, will permit me this!"

Intschu-Tschuna gripped our hands, and said in a heartfelt tone:

"I permit it. You will be not only brothers, but a single man and warrior with two bodies. Howgh!"

Later, at Kleki-Petrah's burial, the bond between the two men is solemnized.

[Chief Intschu-Tschuna] "It was Kleki-Petra's last word and last wish, that Old Shatterhand might be his successor among the warriors of the Apache, and Old Shatterhand swore to him to fulfill with wish. Therefore, he shall be taken up into the tribe of the Apache and be counted as a chief. It shall be as if he had red skin and were born among us. In order for this to be confirmed, he must smoke calumet with every grown warrior of the Apache; but this is not necessary for he will drink Winnnetou's blood, and Winnetou will partake of his; then he will be blood of our blood, and flesh of our flesh. Are the warriors of the Apache in agreement?"

"Howgh, howgh, howgh!" sounded thrice the joyful answer of all present.

"So Old Shatterhand and Winnetou may step up to the coffin, and let their blood drip into the water of brotherhood."

So, a blood-brotherhood, a proper, real blood-brotherhood, about which I had read so often! It is found among many savage and half-savage peoples, and the way it is sealed is that both of the men concerned either mix their blood and drink it, or else the blood is drunk by one man from the other, and also the reverse. The result is that the two are united more firmly, intimately, and unselfishly than if they were brothers by birth.

And here it was that I was to drink Winnetou's blood, and he mine. We arranged ourselves on both sides of the coffin, and Intschu-Tschuna bared the forearm of his son, in order to scratch him with the knife. Out of the small, insignificant cut welled up a few blood drops, which the chief let fall into a cup of water. Then he undertook the same procedure with me, by which some drops fell into another cup. Winnetou received in his hands the cup with my blood, and I the one with his; then said Intschu-Tschuna:

"The soul lives in the blood. May the souls of these two young warriors pass into one another, so that they form one single soul. What Old Shatterhand thinks, be that also Winnetou's thought, and what Winnetou wills, be that also the will of Old Shatterhand. Drink!"

I emptied my cup, and Winnetou his. It was Rio Pecos water with a few drops of blood which one couldn't even taste. Thereupon, the chief took my hand and said:

"You are now the same rank as Winnetou, son of my body, and a warrior of our people. The fame of your deeds will soon be known everywhere, and no other warrior will surpass you. You join us as a chief of the Apache, and as such all branches of our people will honor you!"

As the narrator of the tale, Old Shatterhand reflects on the significance of that bond years after the rite of Apache blood brotherhood actually took place.

And, most strangely, the words of Intschu-Tsucha always proved right, that we would be one soul with two bodies. We understood each other without having to inform one another of our thoughts, feelings, and resolutions. We needed only to look at each other to know exactly what the other one wanted; indeed it was not necessary, and even when we were far apart from one another, we acted with a truly amazing accord, and there never, ever was any sort of disagreement between us. This was not, however, an effect of the partaken blood, but a very natural result of our intimate mutual affection, and of the loving way each of us had become an accustomed part of the views and individual characteristics of the other.

To the modern American reader, some of the translated sentiments above may read as a touch sappy or seem to evoke some sort of repressed homosexual desire between the two men. However, it is important to remember that the story was written by a twice-married heterosexual male, for a heterosexual male audience that continues to identify with and celebrate May's work.

Winnetou and Old Shatterhand are attracted to each other because each man recognizes in the other a matching strength and similar sense of honor. They feel that they are in some way spiritual brothers, that they are somehow *alike* even though their backgrounds are drastically different. Their bond is, above all things, based on a mutual respect for one another as men. This mutual respect actually deepened because the men had several opportunities early in their relationship to compete against each other, test each other, and win each others' respect through honorable action. Their blood-brotherhood is an alliance between formidable, heroic men who see in each other a variation of the self and a worthy comrade.

The excerpts presented above are original translations by Nathan F. Miller. Please see notes for further information.

AN OATH OF SECRECY

FROM MARK TWAIN'S
THE ADVENTURES OF TOM SAWYER

In *The Adventures of Tom Sawyer*, Tom and Huckleberry Finn enter into an emergency blood pact, an oath of secrecy festooned with boyish morbidity and homespun superstition. Because Twain, a.k.a. Samuel Langhorne Clemens, has been so widely read in many translations around the world and in American schools and homes, there can be little doubt that Tom and Huck's pinprick blood bond has been the inspiration for a multitude of solemn playground rites between boys throughout the late nineteenth and twentieth centuries.

The rite takes place late at night in an old tannery, after the boys witness the murder of young Dr. Robinson during a grave robbery. Fearing that the vengeful Injun Joe would surely kill them if they revealed what they saw to anyone, Huck and Tom take the vow of secrecy described in the following excerpt:

After another reflective silence, Tom said:

"Hucky, you sure you can keep mum?"

"Tom, we got to keep mum. You know that. That Injun devil wouldn't make any more of drownding us than a couple of cats, if we was to squeak 'bout this and they didn't hang him. Now, look-a-here, Tom, less take and swear to one another—that's what we got to do—swear to keep mum."

"I'm agreed. It's the best thing. Would you just hold hands and swear that we—"

"Oh no, that wouldn't do for this. That's good enough for little rubbishy common things—specially with gals, cuz they go back on you anyway, and blab if they get in a huff—but there orter be writing 'bout a big thing like this. And blood."

Tom's whole being applauded this idea. It was deep, and dark, and awful; the hour, the circumstances, the surroundings, were in keeping with it. He picked up a clean pine shingle that lay in the moonlight, took a little fragment of "red keel" out of his pocket, got the moon on his work, and painfully scrawled these lines, emphasizing each slow down-stroke by clamping his tongue between his teeth, and letting up the pressure on the up-strokes.

> Huck Finn and
> Tom Sawyer swears
> they will keep mum
> about this and they
> wish they may drop
> down dead in their
> tracks if they ever
> tell and rot.

Huckleberry was filled with admiration of Tom's facility in writing, and the sublimity of his language. He at once took a pin from his lapel and was going to prick his flesh, but Tom said: "Hold on! Don't do that. A pin's brass. It might have verdigrease on it."

"What's verdigrease?"

"It's p'ison. That's what it is. You just swaller some of it once—you'll see."

So Tom unwound the thread from one of his needles, and each boy pricked the ball of his thumb and squeezed out a drop of blood. In time, after many squeezes, Tom managed to sign his initials, using the ball of his little finger for a pen. Then he showed Huckleberry how to make an H and an F, and the oath was complete. They buried the shingle close to the wall, with some dismal ceremonies and incantations, and the fetters that bound their tongues were considered to be locked and the key thrown away.

A figure crept stealthily through a break in the other end of the ruined building, now, but they did not notice it.

"Tom," whispered Huckleberry, "does this keep us from ever telling—always?"

"Of course it does. It don't make any difference what happens, we got to keep mum. We'd drop down dead —don't you know that?"

"Yes, I reckon that's so."

However, the boys do not actually drop down dead when Tom breaks the blood pact in a heroic act of compassion, saving the life of a man falsely accused of Dr. Robinson's murder by acting as the defense's sole witness at the trial. This, even after they had reassured each other and renewed the oath "with dread solemnities." Mostly as the result of luck and distraction, Tom never does reveal that it was Huck who was with him that night in the graveyard.

Huck and Tom's rite follows the pattern of blood-brotherhoods wherein the participants expect some sort of harm to come to them should their bond be broken. However, in this instance, the breaking of the bond itself is an act of courage and moral uprightness. One could assume that, for this reason, the fates gave Tom a pass.

BLOOD + INK

BLOOD AND INK

The Latin word for the tattoo, *stigma*, is derived from a Greek root meaning, roughly, "to prick or sting." Today, the word stigma is usually employed to suggest some sort of infamy — an objectionable burden to bear. Outside of isolated tribal cultures, the tattoo was most often a voluntary or involuntary marker that identified the wearer as a slave, a criminal or a member of a low class. The Greeks and Romans tattooed their slaves and convicts,[1] and the modern tattoo and body modification traditions of Russia[2], India[3] and even Japan[4] can be traced at least partially to the marking of slaves, criminals and members of low social groups. Tattooing has flourished most notably in the West as a pastime among sailors, prisoners and the occasional circus act.

But at some point, the blood and ink trickled down to everyone else.

Today, tattoos are everywhere. Self-proclaimed "modern primitives"[5] have attempted to reclaim older, tribal tattoo motifs, and these seem to have evolved into modern "tribal" designs that, however far removed from anything any primitive tribe ever actually used, look sharp and powerful. Tattoos of this order are favorites of the national god-heroes of America and Europe: our multimillion-dollar sports stars. Designs based on both traditional and modern tattoos are now incorporated into products and graphic design, and are regularly used in major advertising campaigns as visual code for counter-culture coolness. Tattoos are no longer exclusively found on sailors, criminals and freaks; they are also found frequently on sorority girls, frat boys, artists, hippies, avid sports fans, soldiers, cops, rock stars, pop stars, models, actors and actresses, socialites, moms, dads and perfectly respectable grandpas who got a few "in the war."

Even as tattoos have become commonplace — almost mundane — they retain a certain exotic mystique of rebellion, rowdiness and outlaw toughness that is in many cases exactly what makes them attractive. The tattoo is still undoubtedly if sometimes only loosely associated with seafaring men and thugs. Old-fashioned Sailor Jerry-style tattoos are probably more popular than ever among urban hipsters. Bikers and rappers, in addition to popular reality and "investigative infotainment" television programs, have kept images of the tattooed prisoner fresh in the public eye. However, while hand tattoos, facial tattoos, and obscene or overtly confrontational tattoos are still likely to limit one's employment options, simply having a tattoo will no longer banish someone to the fringes of Western society. Perhaps this is the result of commercial commodification or cultural reinforcement. Whatever the reason, tattoos have become a socially acceptable method of customizing the body.

The tattoo now holds a precarious but admirable position in mainstream culture: a tattoo is just naughty enough to be sexy, but not quite naughty enough to throw up any big red flags.

It is this widespread popularity and general social acceptability that makes tattooing especially relevant to this project. Tattoos have become a comfortable, accessible and socially acceptable way for modern men to convey meaningful ideas and commemorate significant events in their lives. And while getting tattooed is by no means an exclusively male pursuit either historically or in everyday modern life, there are powerful cultural associations between tattooing and masculinity in the West. These two factors combined are likely to make tattooing an attractive and culturally consonant way for men to ritualize their bonds in the spirit of blood-brotherhood. The fact that a bit of bloodshed is an inescapable part of getting tattooed drives the association home. If blood-brotherhood is the metaphor, if it is the "what," then the tattoo may prove to be the most popular "how."

THE DEVOTIONAL TATTOO

While it is often assumed that tattooing among Westerners began after Captain Cook's famous first encounters with tribal cultures of New Zealand and Tahiti, there is significant evidence of some pre-existing tattoo traditions among Europeans. Several historians have suggested that tattoos recorded on European and American sailors just a few years after Cook were so distinctly Western in character that they were unlikely to be the result of fascination with exotic cultures, and seem to point to an existing pastime of tattooing among mariners, soldiers and men of lower classes.[6] A.T. Sinclair claimed in 1908 that "Scandinavian deep-water sailors are certainly ninety percent of them tattooed" and that "It is the tradition among them that the custom is very ancient."[7]

One such documented tradition is of particular interest here: The Jerusalem Tattoo. Although it was not referred to as a "tattoo" at the time[8], pilgrims to Jerusalem—as early as the fifteenth century—frequently returned with the date of their pilgrimage[9], various crosses, religious symbols, the name Jerusalem, or the names of Jesus or Mary indelibly marked on their skins.[10] For pious men and women, what was likely a once in a lifetime trip to sacred ground must have been a moving experience of great spiritual significance, and the desire both to record evidence of the occasion and to have themselves forever reminded of their commitment to their god seems completely natural and logical as well as on some level consistent with tribal uses of the tattoo during initiation rites. One Scotsman, William Lithgow, returned home to the court of James I in the seventeenth century with not only the popular Jerusalem Cross, but also some lines of verse tattooed in tribute to his king and a symbol celebrating "the union of the Scottish and English crowns."[11] So here, even in the mid-1600s, well before Cook's eighteenth century voyages, we have evidence of the tattoo being used as an expression of devotion to

God, Crown and Country, in addition to the commemoration of important events in a man's life.

While initiatory and other tribal tattoos no doubt had totemic or religious significance and could be discussed as devotional tattoos in that sense, Lithgow's tattoo signifying allegiance to crown and country reveals another devotional theme in tattooing, especially among men: devotion to a real or artificial kinship group. Because we are discussing blood-brotherhood—a ritualized creation of an alliance or meta-family between two or more men—this sort of devotion is of particular interest. As with blood-brotherhood, devotion to a society, gang, nation or group of men often creates a bond so powerful that it becomes more important than familial bonds.

Lithgow's use of the tattoo to express loyalty and national pride was later echoed in America. Patriotic tattoos, including "flags, eagles, the words 'Independence' and 'Liberty,' [and] '1776'..." surged in popularity with seafaring men during the years immediately following the American Revolution, as the new nation took shape. [12] Flags and eagles remained among the most popular tattoos for U.S. Marines and Navy men through the turn of the century, [13] and were also in evidence among members of Britain's Royal Navy in the 1960s. [14] Samuel Steward also noted a desire among civilians to express devotion to their country of origin or heritage, particularly Mexicans and Irishmen. [15] Among Russian prisoners, devotion to national leaders like Lenin and Stalin was once popular. [16] Nationalistic themes remain commonplace and are easily observable on the arms of military personnel and many others today. However, perhaps equally or more popular is the tattoo used as a sort of tangible evidence of induction into a fraternal order more specific and personal than the loose national "tribe."

Symbols associated with actual fraternal orders, such as the Freemasons, were recorded among the tattoos of sailors as early as the end of the eighteenth century. Indoctrination into the distinct cultures and traditions of the various military branches must certainly be more rigorous and demanding than the leisure-time pursuit of acquiring various initiatory lodge degrees, and the nature of military service itself[17] tends to produce a meaningful sense of devotion to both the military institution and the brotherhood of men who have earned their place as "members." US Marine Corps tattoos such as the "Devil Dog," and various USMC insignia are iconic tattoos, as is the devotional motto, "Semper Fidelis" — Latin for "always faithful." Some men get such tattoos after years of service. But many of these tokens of fidelity to the brotherhood are inked on the arms of new recruits right after completing boot camp, commemorating both the achievement itself and their meaningful vow to be "faithful" to their brothers in arms.

Not all fraternities are as formally organized as the Freemasons or as institutionalized as the military. Some are based on a sense of shared identity and experience. Sailors of all types often found themselves initiated into The Sons of Neptune—a metaphorical fraternity of men who had sailed across the equator. This international tradition dates back at least as far as the nineteenth century, including naval, merchant and civilian sailors. [18] But the "crossing the line" rite was just one expression of the bond between sailors, for whom getting tattooed, often with maritime symbols, became a badge of shared identity and camaraderie. Ira Dye wrote in The Tattoos of Early American Seafarers:

> "...the prime attraction for them was probably that tattooing itself being at this period in America predominantly the province of seafarers, gave them identity with the kinship of seafarers and the world of seafaring. [...] They needed the strength and solidarity of friends and shipmates."

Dye also noted the following line from James Fennimore Cooper's The Pilot: "a messmate before a shipmate, a shipmate before a sailor, a sailor before a stranger." The quotation was popular throughout the nineteenth and early twentieth centuries, and clearly illustrates both the romantic sense of brotherhood observed at least in theory among sailors, and their sense of separateness from their countrymen on land who were more likely to be comforted by wives and families. The on board world of seafaring men was a world apart, a man's world, and getting tattooed in many cases demonstrated a commitment to the fraternity of sailors and to the seafaring life.

Tattoos signifying devotion to lifestyles, ideas and fraternal groups can also be found among gang members and prison inmates—criminals, too, inhabit a male-dominated world apart from the mainstream. The most infamous and visually impressive gang-related tattoos are the legendary full-bodysuit irezumi[19] associated with the Yakuza. Irezumi originated from the marks used to punish criminals during Japan's feudal era. Over time, extensive tattooing became a badge of honor among the gambling bakuto, some of the forerunners of the modern Yakuza. As with Western sailors, these elaborate irezumi served as "a self-inflicted wound that would permanently distinguish the outcasts from the rest of the world." [20] Similar motivations can be found among Russian prisoners. Alix Lambert wrote in Russian Prison Tattoos:

> "When Cain turned public enemy number one, he bore the mark both of his crime and his salvation. The tattoos worn by Russian Federation convicts function in a similar way. On the one hand, they brand the wearer as a murderer, thief, or recidivist. On the other, they make up a criminal coat of arms that confers respect, and therefore protection, in the company of killers."

Spiders and spider webs seem to be almost international symbols of commitment to the criminal life, or to drug addiction. Former Russian military members often wear a striking epaulette tattoo, referencing the uniforms of their previous occupation. Thieves wear "scowling, predatory animals," or cats, and Thieves-in-Law, the leaders of the Russian hierarchy of thieves, have been known to wear elaborate tattoos depicting the crucifixion. Daggers and executioners predictably indicate a murderer or advertise a killer for hire. [21] The tattoo solemnly expresses an "ownership" of one's past actions—for better or worse—and may also advertise his intentions or warn others of his willingness to do harm, like distinctive markings on a poisonous animal.

In modern American prisons, tattoos of gang insignia seal pacts of, in many cases, an unbreakable lifelong devotion to a specific criminal (and often racial) "tribe." Tattoos of gang symbols are reserved for initiated, proven gang members who have sworn oaths of loyalty and have agreed to abide by the gang's honor code. Those who are uninitiated are not allowed to wear similar tattoos; one friend who actually was a prison gang member many years ago told me recently that, "If some guy was claiming to be a member of the gang and wasn't, he'd get beat down and if he had a tat—we'd burn it off." Some sort of initiatory action on behalf of the group is usually required to prove fidelity to the gang before the gang's tattoos can be inscribed on a new recruit's skin. For more casual gangs, this may be something as simple as petty theft, but for hardcore gangs like the Aryan Brotherhood or the Mexican Mafia (La eMe), initiates become full members for life only when they draw blood in an act of extreme violence or murder. No polite resignation from these hardcore gangs is possible; members who attempt to distance themselves from the organization or whose loyalty is questioned are targeted as enemies of the gang. This policy is known among gangs and law enforcement personnel as "Blood in, Blood Out." [22]

Finally, at the far, far lighter end of the spectrum are the devotional tattoos so familiar that they've become a kitschy cultural cliché. The "love" tattoo—whether the object of love is MOM, DAD, a child, or a sweetheart— is a tattoo parlor staple. Sketched records of the tattoos of eighteenth century sailors attest that hearts with initials, like names of lovers carved into a tree trunk, have been traditional in the West for centuries. [23] While undoubtedly the intent here is to provide physical proof of eternal devotion, tattoos of lovers' names are often discouraged by tattoo artists because such inscriptions are too often requested during an emotional haze of romantic or sexual infatuation, and when the romance ends, the tattoo quickly becomes a burden and a visual reminder of a love lost. In an interview with Science Digest in 1945, famed American tattoo artist Charlie Wagner joked that he made the most money changing the names of devotional tattoos:

> "Men come in one week and tell me to put on 'With love, Edith.' Couple of weeks later they come back and say: 'Take off Edith and put in the name of Helen.' " [24]

Fickle though lovers may be, devotional tattoos remain wildly popular and can be seen everywhere, on many different types of men. Nationalistic, tribal and fraternal impulses are frequently localized and expressed via tattoos related to sports teams, high schools or college fraternities. Advances in modern tattoo techniques have made realistic portraits feasible, and it is not uncommon to see a father tattooed with the faces of his children, or a man tattooed with the face of a lost loved one. I once knew a fellow who had the name of his dead brother— along with the date of his suicide— tattooed across his shoulder. Memorial tattoos are a powerful gesture, expressing the sincerest desire to honor the memory of a friend or relative who has passed on. Rather than simply saying, "I will not forget you," the memorial tattoo says, "Our bond meant enough to me that I want to be reminded of you daily, for the rest of my life. I have taken steps to guarantee that you will not be forgotten."

And this is really what the devotional tattoo is truly about.

Sincerity.

The process of tattooing, the pain involved, the permanence of the finished tattoo, the sacrifice of flesh— dedication of space on the body to a person, group or idea— make the tattoo a powerful expression of emotional sincerity. Never mind that tattoos can be

altered, marked over, burned off, grafted over or, now, removed
with lasers. These loopholes have nothing to do with the spirit of
the thing. When someone gets a tattoo dedicated to someone or
something, they mean it to be forever. The tattoo is no superficial
offering of flowers, no ring to be casually slipped off, no mealy-
mouthed oath to be spoken in the moment and forgotten. The
devotional tattoo is a blood oath. The tattoo translates spoken
words into action. It is an active demonstration of sincerity.

It is in part a characteristically male preference for action
over mere expression— to present physical evidence of intent—
that makes getting a tattoo an especially appropriate method for
solemnizing bonds between men.

THE MANLY TATTOO

> Welcome to my life, tattoo
> I'm a man now, thanks to you
>
>   - The Who, "Tattoo" [25]

Gendering the tattoo is no more difficult than assigning a gender
to football, boxing or hunting. In contemporary Western society,
getting tattooed is aesthetically and conceptually a manly endeav-
or. The roots of today's tattoo culture can be traced to seafaring,
military, biker and criminal subcultures, with significant influence
from Japanese sources linked to samurai romanticism and organized crime. The average tattoo parlor until only very recently was
patronized and run primarily by men, with notable but relatively
rare exceptions.

This is not to suggest that women cannot, do not, have not,
or should not get tattooed. Ample photographic evidence
proves that many women were in fact happily and impressively
tattooed over the course of the entire twentieth century. In more
primitive tribal cultures, including the Maori, the Marquesans,
Polynesians, Eskimos and Native Americans, it was commonplace

and sometimes mandatory for both men and women to wear tattoos. Among the Kayans of Borneo, only women can become tattoo artists. Elderly Eskimo women performed the majority of the tattooing among their people, likely because they were expert seamstresses who regularly worked with animal hides. [26] Today, many women are extensively tattooed, including some of my own female friends. Tattooing is now fashionable, and many extremely effeminate males also get tattoos. The point here is not to suggest that getting tattooed is or should be an exclusively masculine tradition. It is rather to underline the fact that tattooing has powerful aesthetic and conceptual associations with manliness in contemporary culture, and to make use of these existing associations by incorporating them into the conceptual architecture of a new tradition specifically designed for two (or more) men.

Conceptual associations with manliness are part of the lore of tattooing—to the extent that getting a tattoo has often served as a rite of passage for men, and that having a tattoo provides visible evidence of toughness and manliness. Just as the permanent nature of tattooing has made it particularly appropriate for expressions of devotion and sincerity, the painful nature of the tattoo process has made getting tattooed something of a "toughness test" in itself. Eighteenth and nineteenth century Japanese firefighters were known to strip to the waist and proudly display their impressive tattoos to convince competing fire brigades that they were real badasses. [27] It's supposed to hurt. That's at least half the point. Tattooist Samuel Steward noted:

> "Many times young men getting a first tattoo asked if the skin could be deadened beforehand, to which they got a joking reply that this was a man's mark they were getting, and they would just have to stand the pain.
>
> Deaden the skin? No, that's not possible. You're not a wimp, are you?" [28]

Due to the current popularity of tattooing—as well as medical advances in fighting infection—tattoo parlors have been modernized and sterilized. They are becoming all-inclusive and visitor friendly. Some exceptionally tony establishments have even been featured on "reality" television shows.[32] Depending on the place and artist, getting a tattoo might feel a bit too much like undergoing some sort of minor outpatient cosmetic surgery.

This is a world away from getting "pricked" on the deck of a man-of-war by some grizzled old salt in between swigs of rum, getting an excruciatingly slow hand poke from a Japanese master, or getting inked with a mixture of soot and urine at the hands of a fellow convict, tucked away in the dark corner of a prison cell. It is this grittier, more dangerous, more painful tradition of tattooing that gives the tattoo its macho character, and places it solidly in the realm of manliness. Even if the usual process has become somewhat less harrowing than it would have been a century ago, worldwide contemporary culture is still saturated with images of exceptionally masculine men who are tattooed. From the iconic Marlboro man to Hell's Angels to today's fighters and football players, the tattoo remains symbolic of maverick toughness. The tattoo communicates physical courage, a show of strength, a willingness to endure pain. Being tattooed is a minor ordeal, in the ritual sense of the word.

The tattoo has a rich historical association with exceptionally masculine men and manly archetypes. This association endures in, and is regularly reinforced by contemporary popular culture. Conceptually, the tattoo is an exercise in self-control, enduring pain, in proving toughness, in actively expressing a man's will on the canvas of his own body. The culture of modern tattooing overflows with masculine metaphor, imagery and iconography, macho slogans—even bawdy male humor.

Using the tattoo to express a bond between men activates these manly associations and employs them to render the distinctly masculine character of that bond. Choosing to solemnize a bond between men in this way says specifically and unequivocally that this is something different, this is something between men.

This book has explored myths and traditions concerning blood-brotherhood, blood oaths and other rites of male alliance as they have been retold and practiced all over the world, spanning most of known human history. While the interest in ritualizing a powerful bond between male friends or allies seems to be a natural outgrowth of male friendship — almost a "human universal" — the specifics of blood-bonding reflect the cultures of the men involved. As smearing blood on a piece of toasted liver and invoking the gods must have seemed like an appropriate gesture in an African village, a mutual or shared tattoo may seem appropriate to many modern men in the West.

For much of history, men have had need to depend on each other for survival. Our luxurious, wealthy bureaucratic modern society offers men a kind of security they have rarely known. Men are encouraged to rely on the State — or even on their wives. Where that security is lacking, where men reject or fail to receive the benefits of modern wealth and luxury — where men are wild — both fraternal bonds and tattooing are especially popular. When (or where) men find that they can no longer rely on or trust the State, when fewer men marry or stay married, when men see themselves as men apart, men may choose to rely on each other. They will look for ways to create brotherhoods and meta-families. Because the tattoo is currently most popular with men who are least invested in the modern bureaucratic society, but also because there is something inherently masculine about it, the shared or mutual tattoo will become an increasingly pervasive way to forge bonds between men.

AFTERWORD

AFTERWORD

CONCERNING THE SECOND EDITION, REVISED
JACK DONOVAN

In 2009, Nathan F. Miller and I released this book as a follow-up to my first book, *Androphilia*. *Blood-Brotherhood and Other Rites of Male Alliance* was originally conceived as a "toolbox for the imagination" intended for homosexual men who disagreed with the idea of "marriage" between two men for various reasons.

However, in our original opening chapters we took great pains to make certain that blood-brotherhood was not portrayed as a homosexual tradition. It is not. Quite the contrary, in fact. All evidence suggests that throughout history it has been heterosexual men, primarily, who have chosen to make blood-brotherhood and swear blood oaths of loyalty to each other. We simply wanted to provide homosexual men who were inclined to solemnize their private relationships with an aesthetically masculine rite that did not borrow from heterosexual marriage rites.

The book reached some of its intended audience, and it made its point. I will continue to make the first edition available to homosexual men who want to read what we called "a survey for androphiles" in its original context. It was an important idea, I think, to show homosexual men a meaningful alternative to merely appropriating and approximating the institution and ceremonies of heterosexual marriages and weddings.

I credit Nathan F. Miller with that idea, and I also credit him with the majority of research that went into this book. His careful work, engaging storytelling and original translations made this book something truly unique.

It is because so much work went into producing this book that I have long wanted to share it with a wider audience. There is still no other cross-cultural survey of material on blood-brotherhood approaching the scope of this book available anywhere, so far as I know. It was a shame to see this fascinating topic passed over by heterosexual men, who understandably assumed that this book wasn't written for them.

As rites of blood-brotherhood have been practiced primarily by heterosexual male friends and allies, this book has as much or more to add to the broader categories of "men's studies" or "male studies" as it did for "gay" studies.

I didn't have to revise much to reformat this book for a broader readership. I may have pulled out ten pages or so, overall. We wrote this book initially with a general male readership in mind. All I had to do was remove parts of the text -- mostly from my own contributions – that directly addressed a homosexual male audience and linked this book to *Androphilia*. Because most the stories contained herein were about heterosexual men to begin with, they didn't have to be changed at all. I hope readers can put aside the fact that they were originally presented to homosexual men, because this collection of blood-brotherhood myths and practices is certainly not about homosexual men.

This is a book about men, and some of the many ways that men have chosen to acknowledge their most important friendships and alliances throughout history.

Jack Donovan
Portland, Oregon
July 2011

NOTES

NOTES

BLOOD BROTHERHOOD

1.   Golding, William, *Lord of the Flies*, Capricorn Books, G.P. Putnam's Sons, 1959, p. 65

2.   Newman, Leslie F., "Notes on Some Rural and Trade Initiation Ceremonies in the Eastern Counties," *Folklore* 51, no. 1, 1940, pp. 32–42

3.   Boyle, John Andrew, "A Eurasian Hunting Ritual," *Folklore* 80, no. 1, 1969, pp. 12–16

4.   Lewis-Williams, J.D, and M Biesele, "Eland Hunting Rituals among Northern and Southern San Groups : Striking Similarities," *Africa: Journal of the International African Institute* 48, no. 2, 1978, pp. 117–134

5.   MacCulloch, John A., *The Religion of the Ancient Celts*, Courier Dover Publications, 2003

6.   Schneider, William M., and Mary Jo Schneider, "Selako Male Initiation," *Ethnology* 30, no. 3, 1991, pp. 279–291

7.   Gilbert, Steve, *Tattoo History: A Source Book*, Juno Books, LLC, 2000

8.   Tiger, Lionel, *Men in Groups,* Random House, 1969

9.   White, Luise, "Blood Brotherhood Revisited: Kinship, Relationship, and the Body in East and Central Africa," *Africa: Journal of the International African Institute*, Vol. 64, No. 3, 1994, p. 359

10.   Lucian, *The Works of Lucian of Samosata: Complete with Exceptions Specified in the Preface*, Translated by Henry Watson Fowler and Francis George Fowler, Clarendon Press, 1905, pp. 56–57, http://books.google.com/

BLOOD BROTHERHOOD IN AFRICA

1.   Tegnaeus, Harry, *Blood-Brothers: An Ethno-Sociological Study of the Institutions of Blood-Brotherhood with Special Reference to Africa*, Philosophical Library, 1952, map on p. 163

2.   Evans-Pritchard, E. E., "Zande Blood-Brotherhood," *Africa: Journal of the International African Institute*, Vol. 6, No. 4, Oct., 1933, p. 370

3.   Ibid., p. 371

4.   Ibid., pp. 375–381

5.   Ibid., pp. 376–377

6.   Ibid., p. 380

7.   Ibid., p. 381

8.   Ibid., pp. 387–388

9.   Ibid., pp. 390–391

10.   Ibid., pp. 397–399

11.   Beidelman, T. O., "The Blood Covenant and the Concept of Blood in Ukaguru," *Africa: Journal of the International African Institute*, Vol. 33, No. 4, Oct., 1963, pp. 324–325

12.   Ibid., p. 325

13.   Ibid.

14.   Ibid., p. 331

15.   Ibid., p. 326

16.   Ibid., pp. 350–351

17.   Ibid., p. 332

18.   Tegnaeus, op. cit., p. 50

19.   Ibid., p. 53

20.   Griffiths, J. B., "Glimpses of a Nyika Tribe (Waduruma),"
The Journal of the Royal Anthropological Institute of Great Britain and Ireland, Vol. 65, Jul. - Dec., 1935, p. 287

21.   Barrett, W. E. H., "Notes on the Customs and Beliefs of
the Wa-Giriama, etc., British East Africa," *The Journal of the Royal Anthropological Institute of Great Britain and Ireland*, Vol. 41, Jan. -
Jun., 1911, p. 35

22.   Tegnaeus, op. cit., p. 67

23.   Ibid., p. 72

24.   Ibid., pp. 109–110

25.   Trumbull, Henry Clay, *The Blood Covenant: A Primitive Rite
and Its Bearings on Scripture*, 2nd ed., J. D. Wattles, 1893, pp. 303–
304

26.   Tegnaeus, op. cit., p. 85

27.   Roscoe, John, *The Baganda: An Account of Their Native
Customs and Beliefs*, MacMillan and Co., 1911, p. 19

28.   Tegnaeus, op. cit., p. 86

29.   White, Luise, "Blood Brotherhood Revisited: Kinship,
Relationship, and the Body in East and Central Africa," *Africa: Journal
of the International African Institute*, Vol. 64, No. 3, 1994, p. 370, note
8

30.   Tegnaeus, op. cit., pp. 86–87

31.   White, op. cit., p. 364

32.   Frazer, James G., "The Mackie Ethnological Expedition to
Central Africa," *Man*, Vol. 20, Jun., 1920, p. 93

33.   Tegnaeus, op. cit., p. 88

34.   Weiss, Brad, "Northwestern Tanzania on a Single Shilling:
Sociality, Embodiment, Valuation," *Cultural Anthropology*, Vol. 12,
No. 3, Aug., 1997, p. 350

35.   Tegnaeus, op. cit., p. 119

36.   Ibid., p. 53

37.   Ibid., p. 122

38.   Ibid., pp. 151–2

39.   Akiga, *The Tiv Tribe as Seen by one of its Members*, Oxford University Press, 1965, pp. 142–143

40.   Tegnaeus, op. cit., pp. 54–56, 62–63

41.   Livingstone, David, *Missionary Travels and Researches in South Africa*, Harper & Bros., 1858, p. 525

42.   Tegnaeus, op. cit., p. 99

43.   Ibid., pp. 78–79

44.   Ibid., p. 97

45.   Ibid., p. 149

46.   Ibid., p. 77

47.   Ibid., pp. 77–78

48.   Griffiths, op. cit., p. 287

49.   Tegnaeus, op. cit., pp. 50–51

50.   Ibid., p. 101

51.   Ibid., p. 85

52.   Ibid., p. 149

53.   Ibid., p. 78

54.   Ibid., p. 80

55.   White, op. cit., p. 363

56.   Tegnaeus, op. cit., pp. 69–70

57.   Ibid., pp., 117–118

58.   Barrett, op. cit., p. 35

59.   Tegnaeus, op. cit., p. 67

60.   Ibid., p. 139

61.   Meyer, Hans; Calder, E. H. S. translator, *Across East African Glaciers: An Account of the First Ascent of Kilimanjaro*, G. Philip & Son, 1891, p. 206

62.   Tegnaeus, op. cit., pp. 103–4

63.   Ibid., p. 65

64.   Ibid., p. 67

65.   Ibid., p. 146

66.   Ibid., p. 53

67.   Ibid., p. 66

68.   Ibid., p. 72

69.   Ibid., p. 90

70.   Ibid., p. 114

71.   Weeks, John H., "Anthropological Notes on the Bangala of the Upper Congo River. (Part III)," *The Journal of the Royal Anthropological Institute of Great Britain and Ireland*, Vol. 40, Jul. - Dec., 1910, p. 360

72.   Tegnaeus, op. cit., p. 103

73.   Ibid., p. 132

74.   Byng-Hall, F. F. W., "Notes on the Bassa Komo Tribe," *Journal of the Royal African Society*, Vol. 8, No. 29, Oct., 1908, p. 18

75.   Tegnaeus, op. cit., p. 137

76.   Ibid.

77.   Ibid., p. 142

78.   Ibid.

79.   Stanley, Henry M., *Through the Dark Continent*, Dover Publications, 1988, Vol. I, p. 387

80.   Cameron, Verney Lovett, *Across Africa*, Daldy, Isbister & Co., 1877, pp. 333–334

81.   Johnstone, H. B., "Notes on the Customs of the Tribes Occupying Mombasa Sub-District, British East Africa," *The Journal of the Anthropological Institute of Great Britain and Ireland*, Vol. 32, Jan.–Jun., 1902, p. 268

82.   Tegnaeus, op. cit., p. 144

83.   Ibid., pp. 74–75

84.   Ward, Herbert, "Ethnographical Notes Relating to the Congo Tribes", *The Journal of the Anthropological Institute of Great Britain and Ireland*, Vol. 24, 1895, pp. 291–292

85.   Tegnaeus, op. cit., p. 104

86.   Ibid., p. 100

87.   White, Luise, op. cit., p. 368

88.   Stanley, Henry M., *The Congo and the Founding of its Free State; a Story of Work and Exploration,* Harper & Brothers, 1885, pp. 104–105

AN AFRICAN FOLKTALE

1.   Lubambula, Y. B., "The Voice of Africa. A Ganda Poem," *Africa: Journal of the International African Institute,* Vol. 18, No. 1, Jan., 1948, pp. 45–48

2.   Williams, F. Lukyn, " Ankole Folk Tales," *Africa: Journal of the International African Institute,* Vol. 21, No. 1, Jan., 1951, pp. 32–40

THE EAGLE AND THE LIZARD

Adapted from T. O. Beidelman's two translations of a Kaguru text. See "The Blood Covenant and the Concept of Blood in Ukaguru," *Africa: Journal of the International African Institute,* Vol. 33, No. 4, Oct., 1963

TRACES FROM THE ANCIENT WORLD

1.   Černý, Jaroslav, "Reference to Blood Brotherhood among Semites in an Egyptian Text of the Ramesside Period," *Journal of Near Eastern Studies,* Vol. 14, No. 3, Jul., 1995, pp. 161–163

2.   Diodorus, *Bibliotheca Historica,* Book 22, sec. 5, par. 1

3.   Xenophon, *Anabasis,* Book 2, sec. 2

4.   Sallust, *Bellum Catilinae,* ch. 22

5.   Tertullian, *Apologeticus,* ch. 9, sec. 9

6.   Codex Justinianus, Digesta, Book 28, sec. 5.59(58)

7.   Herodotus, *Histories,* Book 1, sec. 74

8.   Ibid., Book 3, sec. 8

9.   Athenaeus, *Deipnosophistae,* Book 2, secs. 45–46

10.   Tacitus, *Annales,* Book 12, sec. 47

11.   Valerius Maximus, *Factorum et Dictorum Memorabilium,* Book 9, ch. 11, ext. 3

12.   Herodotus, op. cit. Book 4, sec. 70

13.   Lucian, *Toxaris*, sec. 37

BLOOD-BROTHERHOOD IN NORTHERN AND WESTERN EUROPE

1.   Westermarck, Edward, *The Origin and Development of the Moral Ideas*, Macmillan and Co., 1908, Vol. II, p. 208

2.   Dasent, George Webbe, trans., *The Story of Gisli the Outlaw*, Edmonston and Douglas, 1866, p. 23; Regal, Martin S., trans., "Gisli Sursson's Saga," *The Sagas of Icelanders: a Selection*, Penguin Books, 2001, p. 506

3.   Trumbull, Henry Clay, *The Blood Covenant: a Primitive Rite and its Bearing on Scripture*, John D. Wattles, 1893, 2nd. ed., pp. 41–42

4.   Tegnaeus, Harry, *Blood-Brothers: An Ethno-Sociological Study of the Institutions of Blood-Brotherhood with Special Reference to Africa*, Philosophical Library, 1952, pp. 22–23

5.   Saxo Grammaticus, *Gesta Danorum*, Book I.

6.   Rochholtz, Ludwig Ernst, *Deutscher Glaube und Brauch im Spiegel der heidnischen Vorzeit*, Ferd. Dummler's Verlagsbuchhandlung, 1867, Vol. I, p. 52

7.   Ibid.

8.   Martin Martin, intro. by MacLeod, *A Description of the Western Islands of Scotland*, Eneas Mackay, Stirling, 1934, pp. 41–42, 171; Giraldus Cambrensis, *History and Topography of Ireland*, trans. O'Meara, J., Dolmen Texts, Humanities Press, 1982, p. 108; MacCulloch, J. A., *The Religion of the Ancient Celts*, Kegan Paul, 2005, p. 240

9.   Matthaeus Parisiensis, *English History*, trans. Giles, J. A., 1852, AMS Press, 1968, Vol. I, pp. 30–32

10.   Mills, Charles, *The History of Chivalry; Or, Knighthood and its Times*, Lea and Blanchard, 1844, p. 47

11.   Corley, C., Kennedy, E., *Lancelot of the Lake*, Oxford University Press, 2000, p. 370

12.   Tegnaeus, op. cit., p. 25

13.   Heckethorn, Charles William, *The Secret Societies of All Ages and Countries*, G. Redway, 1897, Vol. I, p. 265

14.   Ibid., p. 266

15.   Tegnaeus, op. cit., p. 27

THE CATTLE RAID OF COOLEY

1.   Dunn, Joseph, translator, *The Ancient Irish Epic Tale Táin Bó Cúalnge*, D. Nutt, 1914, p. 248

2.   Ibid., p. 266

ODIN AND LOKI

Lee M. Hollander, *The Poetic Edda*, (c) Lee M. Hollander 1962, University of Texas Press, Austin, 2nd ed., p. 92

THE VÖLSUNGA SAGA

Hollander, Lee M., trans., Stanza 18 of *Brot af Sigurtharkvidu*, "Fragment of a Sigurd Lay," *The Poetic Edda*, 2nd. ed., revised, University of Texas Press, 6th paperback printing, 1996, p. 246

THE FÓSTBRAEÐRA SAGA

1.   Hollander, Lee Milton, ed. and trans., *The sagas of Kormak and the Sworn brothers,* Princeton University Press for the American-Scandinavian Foundation, 1949, p. 86

2.   Hreinsson, Viðar, ed., *The complete sagas of Icelanders, including 49 tales,* Leifur Eiriksson Pub., 1997, p. 338

DIE GÖTTERDÄMMERUNG

1.   Rochholtz, Ludwig Ernst, *Deutscher Glaube und Brauch im Spiegel der heidnischen Vorzeit,* Ferd. Dummler's Verlagsbuchhandlung, 1867, Vol. I, p. 52

2.   Original English imitative translation for this volume by Nathan F. Miller.

CHAUCER: THE KNIGHT'S TALE

1.   Heather, P. J. "Sworn-Brotherhood," Folklore, Vol. 63, No. 3, Sep., 1952, pp. 158–172

2.   Pratt, Robert A., "Chaucer's Use of the Teseida," PMLA: Publications of the Modern Language Association of America, Vol. 62, No. 3, Sep., 1947, pp. 598–621

CHAUCER: THE PARDONER'S TALE

1.   Canby, Henry Seidel, "Some Comments on the Sources of Chaucer's 'Pardoner's Tale'," *Modern Philology*, Vol. 2, No. 4, Apr., 1905, pp. 477–487

THE OUTLAWS OF INGLEWOOD FOREST

Child's title of the ballad names the protagonists, being "Adam Bell, Clym of the Cloughe and Wyllyam of Cloudeslee." Despite the age of the ballad, its language is still enjoyably rather clear to modern readers. A good online source for this and the other Child ballads is at http://www.sacred-texts.com/neu/eng/child/ch116.htm.

CENTRAL AND EASTERN EUROPE

1.   Tegnaeus, Harry, Blood-Brothers: *An Ethno-Sociological Study of the Institutions of Blood-Brotherhood, with Special Reference to Africa, Philosophical Library,* 1952, p. 26

2.   Joinville, John, *The Life of Saint Louis*, trans. Hague, Rene', Sheed and Ward, 1955, pp. 150–151

3.   Ciszewski, Stanisław, *Künstliche Verwandstschaft bei den Südslaven*, Berlag des Verfassers, 1897, pp. 44–45

4.   Ibid., pp. 65–66

5.   Krauss, Friedrich, *Sitte und Brauch der Südslaven*, Alfred Hölder, 1885, p. 628

6.   Ciszewski, op. cit., pp. 61–62

7.   Ibid., p. 62

8.   Georgevitch, Tih. R., "Serbian Habits and Customs," *Folklore*, Vol. 28, No. 1, Mar. 31, 1917, p. 47

9.   Foley, John Miles, "Strategies for Translating Serbo-Croatian Traditional Oral Narrative," *Journal of Folklore Research*, Vol. 28, No. 1, Jan.– Apr., 1991, p. 79, note 13

10.   Coon, Carlton S., *A Reader in Cultural Anthropology*, R. E. Krieger Pub. Co., 1948, p. 369

11.   Ciszewski. op. cit., pp. 15, 61

12.   Ibid., pp. 63–64

13.   Pethahiah, William Ainsworth, *Travels of Rabbi Petachia*, trans. Benisch, Abraham, Messrs. Trubner & Co., 1856, p. 5

14.   Ciszewski, op. cit., p. 67

15.   Ibid., p. 26

PRINCE MARKO

1.   Tegnaeus, Harry, *Blood-Brothers: An Ethno-Sociological Study of the Institutions of Blood-Brotherhood with Special Reference to Africa*, Philosophical Library, 1952, pp. 27–28

2.   Petrovitch, Woislav M., *Hero Tales and Legends of the Serbians*, Frederick A. Stokes Company, 1915, p. 90

THE RUSSIAN BOGATYRS

1.   Cavendish, Richard, ed., *Legends of the World*, Orbis, 1982, p. 294

2.   Chadwick, N. Kershaw, *Russian Heroic Poetry*, Russell & Russell Inc., 1964, p. 90

BLOOD RITUALS OF THE ARABS

1.   Herodotus, *Histories*, Book 3, sec. 8

2.   Trumbull, Henry Clay, *The Blood Covenant: A Primitive Rite and Its Bearings on Scripture*, 2nd ed., J. D. Wattles, 1893, pp. 5–8, 10–11, 235

3.   Smith, William Robertson, *Kinship and Marriage in Early Arabia*, Cambridge, University Press, 1885, pp. 48–49

4.   Ibid., p. 51

5.   Tegnaeus, Harry, *Blood-Brothers: An Ethno-Sociological Study of the Institutions of Blood-Brotherhood, with Special Reference to Africa*, Philosophical Library, 1952, p. 31

6.   Wellhausen, Julius, *Reste Arabischen Heidentums*, G. Reimer, 1897, pp. 125–126

7.   Doughty, Charles M., *Travels in Arabia Deserta*, Boni and Liveright, 1921, Vol. 2, pp. 40–41

THE EPIC OF GILGAMESH

Kovacs, Maureen, *The Epic of Gilgamesh,* Stanford University Press, 1989, p. 37

BLOOD OATHS AND SWORN BROTHERHOOD IN ASIA

1.   Gorer, Geoffrey, *Himalayan Village*, 2nd ed., Basic Books, 1967, pp. 118–119

2.	Francke, August Hermann, *A Lower Ladakhi version of the Kesar saga*, Asian Educational Services, 2000, p. 485

3.	Orléans, H. P. M., Bent, H., *From Tonkin to India by the sources of the Irawadi*, January '95–January '96, Dodd, Mead, & Co., 1898, p. 235

4.	Okada, Ferdinand, "Ritual Brotherhood: A Cohesive Factor in Nepalese Society," *Southwestern Journal of Anthropology*, Vol. 13, No. 3., Autumn, 1957, pp. 212–217

5.	Minns, Ellis Hovell, *Scythians and Greeks*, Cambridge University Press, 1913, pp. 92–93

6.	Serruys, Henry, "A Note on Arrows and Oaths among the Mongols," *Journal of the American Oriental Society*, Vol. 78, No. 4, Oct. – Dec., 1958, p. 289

7.	Weatherford, Jack, *Genghis Khan and the Making of the Modern World*, Three Rivers Press, 2004, p. 22

8.	Schram, Louis M. J., "The Monguors of the Kansu-Tibetan Frontier. Their Origin, History, and Social Organization," *Transactions of the American Philosophical Society*, New Series, Vol. 44, No. 1, 1954, p. 106

9.	Ibid., p. 107

10.	ter Haar, Barend, J., *Ritual and Mythology of the Chinese Triads : Creating an Identity*, Koninklije Brill NV, 1998, pp. 151–152

11.	Ibid., pp. 152–153

12.	Ibid., pp. 156–158

13.	Ibid., pp. 159–161

14.	Ibid., pp. 161–164

15.	Ibid., p. 166

16.	Ibid., pp. 167–169

17.	Ibid., pp. 180–195

18.	Harrell, Stevan, *Ploughshare Village, Culture and Context in Taiwan*, University of Washington Press, 1982, pp. 128–130

19.	Schram, op. cit., p. 106

20.   Trumbull, Henry Clay, *The Blood Covenant: a Primitive Rite and its Bearing on Scripture*, John D. Wattles, 1893, 2nd. ed., pp. 313–314

21.   Ibid., p. 316

22.   Ibid.

23.   Tegnaeus, Harry, *Blood-Brothers: An Ethno-Sociological Study of the Institutions of Blood-Brotherhood with Special Reference to Africa, Philosophical Library*, 1952, p. 34

24.   Hickey, Gerald Cannon, *Shattered World: Adaptation and Survival among Vietnam's Highland Peoples during the Vietnam War*, University of Pennsylvania Press, 1993, p. 59

25.   Ibid., pp 119–120

26.   Ibid., p. 151

27.   Paik, George L., *The History of Protestant Missions in Korea*, Union Christian College Press, 1929, pp. 15–16

28.   *Chosun Ilbo* newspaper, digital English edition, "A Boy From Sangmori / Blood Brother Kim Sam-soo," Jan. 16, 1998, Copyright (c)2004 DIGITAL CHOSUN, http://english.chosun.com/w21data/html/news/199801/199801160350.html

29.   Masujima, R., "On the *Jitsuin* or Japanese Legal Seal," *Transactions of the Asiatic Society of Japan*, The Asiatic Society of Japan, 1889, vol. XVII, pp. 103–104.

30.   Louis-Frédéric; Roth, K., *Japan Encyclopedia*, illustrated edition, Harvard University Press, 2005, p. 511

GENGHIS KHAN

1.   Serruys, Henry, "A Note on Arrows and Oaths among the Mongols," *Journal of the American Oriental Society*, Vol. 78, No. 4, Oct.–Dec., 1958, pp. 289–290

2.   Waley, Arthur, The Secret History of the Mongols and other pieces, Barnes & Noble, 1963, p. 235

3.   Ibid., p. 242

4.   Ibid., p. 283

5.   Selyanov, Sergei. Melnik, Anton. (Producers), & Sergey. Bodrov. (Director). (2008). *Mongol.* DVD. Warner Home Video.

THE ROMANCE OF THE THREE KINGDOMS

1.   Luo, Guanzhong, *Three kingdoms : a historical novel*, trans. Roberts, Moss; Foreign Languages Press; University of California Press, 1995. pp. 12–13

2.   Weller, Robert, P., "Sectarian Religion and Political Action in China," *Modern China*, Sage Publications, Vol. 8, No. 4, Oct., 1982, p. 470

LEGENDARY ORIGINS OF THE TIANDIHUI

1.   For a detailed investigation of the truth behind the legend, see Murray, Dian H., *The origins of the Tiandihui : the Chinese triads in legend and history*, Stanford University Press, 1994.

2.   Ward, J. S. M.; Stirling, W. G., *Hung Society Or the Society of Heaven and Earth*, Baskerville Press, Ltd., 1925, p. 42

FEI WEI AND CHI CH'ANG

1.   Lieh Tzu, *The Book of Lieh Tzu*, trans. Graham, A. C., Murray, 1960, pp. 112–113.

THE THREE SWORN BROTHERS: A CHINESE FOLKTALE

1.   This telling of the tale is adapted from "The Three Sworn Brothers," from *Chinese Nights' Entertainment*, by Adele M. Fielde, G.P. Putnam's sons, 1893.

THE FOUR SWORN BROTHERS: A KOREAN FOLK TALE

In-sob, Zong, *Folk Tales from Korea*, Hollym International Corp., 3rd ed., pp.162-166

THE TATENOKAI BLOOD OATH

1.   Mishima, Yukio, *Sun & Steel,* Trans. John Bester, New York, Kodansha International, 1970.

2.   Stokes, Henry Scott, *The Life and Death of Yukio Mishima,* New York, Alfred A. Knopf, 1974.

3.   Mishima, Yukio, *Runaway Horses,* Trans. Michael Gallagher, New York, Alfred A. Knopf, 1973   (Original Work Published 1970)

BLOOD RITUALS OF AUSTRALIA AND THE PACIFIC ISLANDS

1.   Spencer, Baldwin; Gillen, F. J., *The Arunta, A Study of a Stone Age People*, Anthropological Publications, 1966, p. 482

2.   Hassell, Ethel; Davidson, D. S., "Myths and Folk-Tales of the Wheelman Tribe of South-Western Australia: IV," *Folklore*, Vol. 46, No. 3, Sep., 1935, pp. 268–269, 271, 279

3.   Toy, Crawford H., *Introduction to the History of Religions*, Ginn and Co., 1913, p. 74

4.   Needham, Rodney, "A Note on the Blood Pact in Borneo," *Man*, Royal Anthropological Institute of Great Britain and Ireland, Vol. 54., Jun., 1954, pp. 90–91

5.   Tegnaeus, Harry, *Blood-Brothers: An Ethno-Sociological Study of the Institutions of Blood-Brotherhood with Special Reference to Africa*, Philosophical Library, 1952, p. 38

6.   Ibid., p. 36

7.   Ellis, William, *History of Madagascar*, London, Fisher, Son and Co., 1838, Vol. 1, p. 191, note.

8.   Forbes, H. O., "On Some of the Tribes of the Island of Timor," *The Journal of the Anthropological Institute of Great Britain and Ireland*, Royal Anthropological Institute of Great Britain and Ireland, Vol. 13, 1884, pp. 426

9.   Bastian, Adolf, *Indonesien; oder, die Inseln des malayischen Archipel*, Ferd. Dümmlers Verlagsbuchhandlung, 1884, Vol. IV, p. 65

10.   Tegnaeus, op. cit., p. 38

11.   Ibid.

12.   Ibid., p. 39

13.   Major, Henry R., *Early Voyages to Terra Australis*, Hakluyt Society, 1859, p. 92

14.   Hagen, Bernard, *Unter den Papua's*, Wiesbaden, C. W. Kreidel's Verlag, 1899, p. 262

15.   Gorodzov, V. A., "The Typological Method in Archaeology," *American Anthropologist*, New Series, Vol. 35, No. 1, Jan.–Mar., 1933, p. 97

16.   Ober, Frederick, A., *Ferdinand Magellan*, Harper & Brothers, 1907, p. 205

17.   Ibid., p. 220

18.   Pigafetta, Antonio, *The Voyage of Magellan; the Journal of Antonio Pigafetta*, trans. Paige, Paula S., Prentice-Hall, 1969, p., 83

19.   Ibid., pp. 87–88

20.   Barrows, David P., *History of the Philippines*, American Book Company, 1905, pp. 127–128

21.   Foreman, John, *The Philippine Islands*, Charles Scribner's Sons, 1906, p. 365

THE NAME EXCHANGE –"THE HEATHEN"

1.   Dorson, Richard M. ed., *Peasant Customs and Savage Myths*, Vol. I, University of Chicago Press, 1968, pp. 383–384

2.   Radcliffe-Brown, A. R., "On Joking Relationships," *Africa: Journal of the International African Institute*, Vol. 13, No. 3, Jul., 1940, pp. 207–208

3.   Haddon, Alfred C., "The Ethnography of the Western Tribe of Torres Straits," *The Journal of the Anthropological Institute of Great Britain and Ireland*, Vol. 19, 1890, p. 405

4.   Rivers, W. H. R., "A Genealogical Method of Collecting Social and Vital Statistics," *The Journal of the Anthropological Institute of Great Britain and Ireland*, Vol. 30, 1900, p. 77

5.   Fox, C. E., "Social Organization in San Cristoval, Solomon Islands," *The Journal of the Royal Anthropological Institute of Great Britain and Ireland*, Vol. 49, Jan., 1919, p. 138

6.   Heinrich, Albert; Anderson, Russell L., "Some Formal Aspects of a Kinship System," *Current Anthropology*, Vol. 12, No. 4/5, Oct., 1971, p. 552

7.   Kirkpatrick, John, "Taure'are'a: A Liminal Category and Passage to Marquesan Adulthood," *Ethos*, Vol. 15, No. 4, Dec., 1987, pp. 392

8.   Maranda, Pierre, "Marquesan Social Structure: An Ethnohistorical Contribution," *Ethnohistory*, Vol. 11, No. 4, Autumn, 1964, pp. 348

9.   Porter, David, *Journal of a Cruise Made to the Pacific Ocean*, Wiley & Halsted, 1822, p. 68

10.   Wagner, Henry R., *Sir Francis Drake's Voyage Around the World*, John Howell Books, 1926 pp. 145–146

11.   Watson, Lillian Eichler, *The Customs of Mankind*, Doubleday, inc., 1924, pp.154–155

BLOOD RITUALS AND BROTHERHOOD IN THE AMERICAS

1.   Mandelbaum, David G., "Friendship in North America," *Man*, Vol. 36, Dec., 1936, p. 206

2.   Tegnaeus, Harry, *Blood-Brothers: An Ethno-Sociological Study of the Institutions of Blood-Brotherhood, with Special Reference to Africa, Philosophical Library*, 1952, p. 41.

3.   Bancroft, Hubert Howe, *The Native Races of the Pacific States of North America*, A. L. Bancroft & Co., 1883, Vol. 1, pp. 636–637

4.   Trumbull, Henry Clay, *The Blood Covenant: A Primitive Rite and Its Bearings on Scripture*, 2nd. ed., J. D. Wattles, 1893, p. 54

5.   Bancroft, op. cit., pp. 740–741

6.   Wilbert, Johannes, "Kinship and Social Organization of the Yekuána and Goajiro," *Southwestern Journal of Anthropology*, Vol. 14, No. 1, Spring, 1958, p. 55.

7.   Southey, Robert, *History of Brazil*, B. Franklin, 1970, Vol. 1, p. 250

8.   Faron, Louis C., "Symbolic Values and the Integration of Society among the Mapuche of Chile," *American Anthropologist*, New Series, Vol. 64, No. 6, Dec., 1962, p. 1156

9.   Latcham, Richard E., "The Totemism of the Ancient Andean Peoples," The Journal of the Royal Anthropological Institute of Great Britain and Ireland, Vol. 57, Jan. – Jun., 1927, pp. 59–63, 81

MASHTINNA

This telling is adapted from "The Comrades," *Wigwam Evenings: Sioux Folk Tales Retold* Little, Brown, and Company, 1909, by Dr. Charles Alexander Eastman (Ohiyesa), and Mary Nancy Eastman.

WINNETOU AND OLD SHATTERHAND

The long quotations presented here were translated from the original German by Nathan F. Miller.

This translation was compared to the Marion Ames Taggart translation, published by Benziger Brothers in 1898, which is believed to be in the public domain.

May, Karl Friedrich. *Winnetou.* Translated by Marion Ames Taggart. Benziger Brothers. 235 pp. Original from Harvard University. Digitized September 21, 2007. Accessed via Google Books.

Biographical information about Karl May and background information about his book, *Winnetou* was summarized from David Koblick's

"Introduction" and Richard H. Cracroft' s"Foreword" to Koblick's Washington State University Press translation of *Winnetou*. This was also the translation that was initially consulted for content.

May, Karl Friedrich. *Winnetou*. Translated and abridged by David Koblcik from the original 1892-93 edition of Winnetou I: foreword by Richard H. Cracroft. Washington State University Press. 1999.

BLOOD AND INK

1.   Jones, C.P., "Stigma and Tattoo," *Written on the Body*, Caplan, Jane (ed.), Reaktion Books, 2000

2.   Schrader, Abby, "Branding the Other/Tattooing the Self," *Written on the Body*, Caplan, Jane (ed.), Reaktion Books, 2000

3.   Anderson, Clare, "Godna: Inscribing Indian Convicts in the Nineteenth Century," *Written on the Body*, Caplan, Jane (ed.), Reaktion Books, 2000

4.   Gilbert, Steve, *Tattoo History – A Sourcebook*, Juno Books, 2000

5.   Vale, V. *Modern Primitives*, RE/Search Publications, 1989

6.   Dye, op. cit., p. 522.; Caplan, op. cit., "Introduction," pp. xi-xxiii

7.   Sinclair, A.T., "Tattooing – Oriental and Gypsy," *American Anthropologist*, New Series. Vol. 10, No. 3, Jul. - Sep., 1908, p. 367

8.   Historians generally agree that the word "tattoo" was undeniably popularized by Cook, who first recorded the Tahitian word *tatau* as "tattaw" in his diaries in 1769.

9.   Sinclair, op. cit., p. 363

10.   Fleming, Juliet, "The Renaissance Tattoo," *Written on the Body*. p. 79

11.   Ibid., p. 80

12.   Dye, op. cit., p. 541

13.   Farenholt, A, "Some Statistical Observations Concerning Tattooing As Seen By The Recruiting Surgeon," U.S. Naval Medical Bulletin, Vol.7, No.1, 1913. p. 101

14.   Scutt, R.W.B.; Gotch, Christopher, Art, *Sex and Symbol – The Mystery of Tattooing*, A.S. Barnes and Co., 1974. p. 97

15.   Steward, op. cit., p. 86

16.   Lambert, Alix, *Russian Prison Tattoos, Codes of Authority, Domination and Struggle*. Schiffer Publishing, 2003

17.   Tiger, Lionel, *Men in Groups*. Random House, 1969. This note is provided only for those readers who are interested in exploring the general theme of male bonding through aggression. The military provides an environment designed to encourage male bonding through aggression on the largest possible scale, taking advantage of some of the natural tendencies of human men that Tiger (who coined the phrase "male bonding" in this book) eloquently described. For layman-friendly elaboration on the idea of the "hunting ape" that rings true 40 years later, I highly recommend: Morris, Desmond, *The Naked Ape*, Random House, 1967.

18.   Any search for "Crossing the Line" will bring up multiple descriptions of this "secret" rite. There are some great photos in Steven Zeeland's *Sailors and Sexual Identity*. I also found some 19th century descriptions in *Rites and Passages* by Margaret S. Creighton.

19.   Also "Horimono." *Irezumi* is considered a more vulgar term for the tattoo, because it is associated historically with tattooing used for punishment, whereas *horimono* refers to the tattoo as art. The words are being used more interchangeably in Japan today, but *irezumi* seemed more appropriate here. Kitamura, Takahiro; Kitamura, Katie M., *Bushido – Legacies of the Japanese Tattoo*, Schiffer Publishing, 2001, p. 106

20.   Kaplan, David E.; Dubro, Alec., *Yakuza – Japan's Criminal Underworld*, University of California Press, 2003

21.   Lambert, quotation p. 16, information regarding the meaning of tattoos found in pictures and captions throughout.

22.   Valentine, Bill, *Gangs and Their Tattoos – Identifying Gangbangers on the Street and In Prison*, Paladin Press, 2000

23.   Dye, op. cit., p. 529

24.   Gilbert, op. cit., p. 133, (Original source: Anonymous, "An Old Tattooer Talks Shop," *Science Digest*, March 1945, p. 22)

25.   Townshend, Pete, "Tattoo," Lyrics, *The Who Sell Out*. Track (UK), 1967

26.   Gilbert, op. cit.

27.   Kitamura, op. cit., p. 15.

28.   Steward, op.cit., p. 57, (Bolding mine.)

THE AUTHORS

NATHAN F. MILLER

Born in 1968 in Berea, Ohio, Nathan F. Miller grew up in the Kinzua Highlands region of northwestern Pennsylvania. He attended the University of Pittsburgh, studying computer science, and Japanese language and culture. He has been a school custodian, computer programmer, dishwasher, freelance translator, and presently works in the home improvement industry. He lives in Southwestern Pennsylvania. This is his first book.

Nathan would like to thank Russell J. Parkinson for makng critical comments on some of the initial sections of this book. He would also like to thank Matt Moody for his close editing of all of the book's chapters. He would like to thank his family for their moral support during the writing of this book. He would especially like to thank Lee W. Kikuchi and Randall D. Christner for the substantial help they gave him during the trying times he faced while this book was being completed. Nathan would like to thank Jack Donovan for all the work he did to help bring this book to reality, and for initially inspiring him to express his blood-brotherhood idea in literary form.

JACK DONOVAN

Jack Donovan moonlights as an advocate for the resurgence of tribalism and manly virtue. He has contributed articles to *Alternative Right, The Spearhead, The Hall of Manly Excellence, Counter-Currents*, and *Amerika*.

Donovan has appeared on television and radio to discuss the topic of manhood, and in 2010 spoke to a group of students at a private high school about "Masculinity in the 21st Century." His first book, *Androphilia*, can be found in libraries across the world, and in 2009 Donovan (as Malebranche) also appeared in the documentary feature *The Butch Factor*, directed by Christopher Hines. Androphilia has been read and discussed by several college sociology and human sexuality classes.

Author Roosh Vorek named Donovan's third book, *The Way of Men*, "Best Book of 2012 for Men." Sam Sheridan, author of A Fighter's Heart, called it "...a thought-provoking treatise on the essential struggle of men."

Jack Donovan is originally from rural Pennsylvania. He has lived and worked in New York City, Los Angeles, San Francisco, San Diego and currently resides in Portland, Oregon.

In preparation for this book, Donovan and his compadre Lucio became made blood-brotherhood in a mutual tattooing ritual.

FOR ESSAYS, NEWS, AND REVIEWS

JACK-DONOVAN.COM

ALSO BY JACK DONOVAN

2007   ANDROPHILIA

2012   THE WAY OF MEN

ALSO FROM DISSONANT HUM

2012   ALL ABOUT WOMEN
        BY SIMON SHEPPARD

DISSONANT HUM

2013

CPSIA information can be obtained
at www.ICGtesting.com
Printed in the USA
BVHW080753291220
596445BV00003B/227

9 780985 452322